PEARSON

my World GEOGRAPHY

ASSESSMENT HANDBOOK

IN PRINT AND ONLINE AT
myworldgeography.com

• Includes two assessments for every chapter

• Provides rubrics to establish criteria for assessment

• Helps monitor adequate yearly progress using benchmark tests

• Prepares students for end-of-course exams

PEARSON

Boston, Massachusetts
Chandler, Arizona
Glenview, Illinois
Upper Saddle River, New Jersey

PEARSON

ISBN-13: 978-0-13-363802-8

ISBN-10:   0-13-363802-2

1 2 3 4 5 6 7 8 9 10 V031 14 13 12 11 10

Contents

Contents

Analyzing Multiple-Choice Questions

Multiple-choice questions can be tricky, so be sure to read the question and all of the answer choices before you choose the best answer. These five steps can help you answer a multiple-choice question correctly.

Steps for Analyzing a Multiple-Choice Question

STEP 1 Carefully read the stem. Read through the entire question before choosing an answer.

STEP 2 Note key words, clues, or absolutes in the question or stem. Identify any key words that can be used as clues. Identify any absolutes, and note how they limit possible answers.

STEP 3 Read *all* the possible answers carefully. Read each possible answer for words or phrases that make it incorrect.

STEP 4 Eliminate answers that are obviously wrong. Narrow your list of possible choices.

STEP 5 Select the choice that correctly answers the question or completes the statement. The best answers should be a complete and accurate response to the stem.

> **Quick Tip**
> *Be sure to read the entire question before choosing an answer.*

Answer the following questions using the steps to analyze multiple-choice questions. Write your answers on a separate sheet of paper.

1. As feudalism ended and trade increased, Europe found itself in a time of renewed interest in art and learning, called the
   A Catholic Reformation.
   B Inquisition.
   C Renaissance.
   D Reformation.

2. Thomas Newcomen and James Watt both invented
   A electric light bulbs.
   B gravity detectors.
   C navigation instruments.
   D steam engines.

3. Which king believed so strongly in absolutism that he said, "L'état, c'est moi"?
   A Louis XIV of France
   B Philip II of Spain
   C King Augustus II of Poland
   D Henry VIII of England

4. Which countries were members of the Axis Powers during World War II?
   A the United States, Germany, and France
   B Japan, Italy, and Britain
   C Britain, France, and the United States
   D Germany, Italy, and Japan

Identifying the Main Idea in a Reading Passage

Good readers are like detectives. They look for clues that reveal the main idea of a passage. The main idea is the message the writer wants you to remember. Learn how to recognize the main idea of a reading passage before answering test questions by following these steps.

Steps for Identifying the Main Idea in a Reading Passage

STEP 1 Read the title of the passage. The title often gives you an idea of what the passage is about.

STEP 2 Identify the topic sentence. Skim the passage to find the topic sentence, which often appears at the beginning or end of a passage.

STEP 3 Read the passage carefully. Pay close attention to what it says.

STEP 4 Identify supporting details. Notice how the details relate to the topic sentence.

STEP 5 Write one sentence that states the main idea in your own words. Make sure your main idea statement relates to all of the supporting details.

Quick Tip
Skimming means reading quickly while looking for key words that indicate time, cause-and-effect relationships, or comparisons.

Read the following passage. Use the steps to identify the main idea of the passage. Then write one sentence that states the main idea in your own words on a separate sheet of paper.

British Government

You have read about King John signing the Magna Carta in 1215. This document limited the power of the king and gave rights to his people. It was the beginning of democratic government in England. Today, the British government is a constitutional monarchy. This means the monarch is the ceremonial leader, but Parliament makes the laws. Unlike the U.S. Constitution, the British constitution is not a single document, but a group of laws and court decisions. The ceremonial leader is Queen Elizabeth II, who serves as a symbol of Britain's nationhood.

Understanding and Interpreting Bar Graphs

Some test questions require you to read a bar graph. A bar graph is a simple, clear way to visually represent information that can be difficult to understand in written form. The five steps below will help you understand and interpret bar graphs. Follow these steps when you answer test questions that include bar graphs.

Steps for Understanding and Interpreting Bar Graphs

STEP 1 Read the title of the bar graph. Read the graph title to determine its topic.

STEP 2 Read the labels. Read the labels for the horizontal axis and the vertical axis.

STEP 3 Read the key that appears on the bar graph. The key indicates what is being represented.

STEP 4 Read the test question about the bar graph. Read through the entire question.

STEP 5 Choose the best answer. Decide which multiple-choice option best fits your answer from Step 4.

> **Quick Tip**
> *Be sure to read the labels on the graph and the key.*

Use the above steps to answer the following questions. Write your answers on a separate sheet of paper.

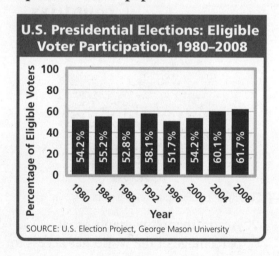

U.S. Presidential Elections: Eligible Voter Participation, 1980–2008

SOURCE: U.S. Election Project, George Mason University

1. What is the title of the graph?
2. What labels are on the horizontal and vertical axis?
3. According to the graph, what percentage of eligible voters participated in the 2000 election?
   A 61.7%
   B 60.1%
   C 54.2%
   D 58.1%

Understanding and Interpreting Line and Circle Graphs

Line graphs and circle graphs are simple, clear ways to visually show information. When you break down the process of interpreting graphs into steps, you can analyze the information shown in them and correctly answer test questions.

> ***Steps for Understanding Line and Circle Graphs***
>
> **STEP 1 Read the title of the graph.** The graph title helps you understand the topic.
>
> **STEP 2 Identify the key.** This information can help you interpret what is shown. Examine the colors, patterns, and shading in the key, and study how they are represented in the graph.
>
> **STEP 3 Identify any symbols or labels.** Read the labels, and make sure that you understand what each represents.
>
> **STEP 4 Identify the graph's main idea.** Put the main idea of the graph in your own words.

> **Quick Tip**
> *Be sure to read the labels on the graph and on the key.*

Use the above steps to answer the following questions. Write your answers on a separate sheet of paper.

Average Temperatures

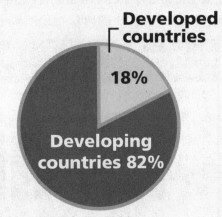

World Population, 2008

Developed countries

18%

Developing countries 82%

SOURCE: UN Population Division

1. According to the graph, what is the average yearly temperature in March for this city?
   A 80°F   C 60°F
   B 55°F   D 70°F

2. According to the graph, what percentage of the world has access to a good education?
   A 100%   C 18%
   B 82%   D 28%

Analyzing a Chart or Table

Charts and tables organize large amounts of information into columns and rows. This makes it easier to compare and analyze large amounts of information.

Steps for Analyzing a Chart or Table

STEP 1 Read the title. The title describes the general information included in the chart or table.

STEP 2 Identify the column and subcolumn headings. A column heading is the word or words at the top of each vertical column of information. Sometimes charts and tables have subcolumn headings at different levels.

STEP 3 Read the information in each cell. A row is the information that is presented horizontally in the table. A cell is the intersection of a column and a row.

STEP 4 Determine the relationship among the chart or table entries. Compare and contrast the information.

> **Quick Tip**
> *Rows present information from left to right, and columns present information from top to bottom.*

Using the steps above, evaluate the chart and answer the questions. Write your answers on a separate sheet of paper.

Famous People of the Greek Classical Age		
Person	**Famous For**	**Lived**
Aeschylus	Playwright	about 525 B.C. to 456 B.C.
Pericles	Athenian general; made Athens more democratic	495 B.C. to 429 B.C.
Herodotus	Historian	about 484 B.C. to c. 425 B.C.
Socrates	Philosopher	469 B.C. to 399 B.C.
Euripides	Playwright	about 480 B.C. to 406 B.C.
Alexander	King of Macedonia; conqueror of great empire	356 B.C. to 323 B.C.
Thucydides	Historian	about 460 B.C. to about 395 B.C.
Aristophanes	Playwright	about 448 B.C. to 330 B.C.

1. What is the title of this chart?
2. What information is given in each of the columns?
3. What was Alexander famous for?
4. Which famous Greeks were historians?

Analyzing a Map for a Multiple-Choice Question

Multiple-choice questions on a test will sometimes require you to use a map to answer the question. Different parts of the map will help you choose the correct response. Knowing how to read the map will help you find that correct response.

Steps for Analyzing a Map for a Multiple-Choice Question

STEP 1 Identify the map's title, key, scale, and compass rose. The map's title, key, scale, and compass rose help you determine what the map shows.

> **Quick Tip**
> *Always read the map title first.*

STEP 2 Determine what kind of information the map presents. Ask yourself: What is the main type of information on the map?

STEP 3 Read the multiple-choice question. Read through the entire question before choosing an answer.

STEP 4 Decide what part of the map will help you find the answer. Think about the question while looking at the map closely.

STEP 5 Answer the question in your own words without looking at the answer choices. This step will help you locate possible answers.

STEP 6 Eliminate the choices that are obviously wrong. Narrow your list of possible choices further.

STEP 7 Choose the best answer. Choose the best answer that correctly responds to the question.

Use the maps and the steps to answer the following questions. Write your answers on a separate sheet of paper.

1. What does this map show?
   A A man-made lake
   B A mountain range across North Africa
   C A delta created by soil carried by the Nile
   D Political boundaries of countries in North Africa

Rubric for Assessing a Report

Grading Criteria	Excellent	Acceptable	Minimal	Unacceptable
Content	Contains many relevant key facts and details; completely and concisely meets requirements; informative graphic organizers.	Contains sufficient facts and details to complete the assignment; includes graphic organizers.	Many necessary facts and details are present; contains some unimportant information.	Important facts and details are missing; much information is irrelevant.
Use of Resources	Uses a range of primary and secondary (six or more); correctly documents organizers.	Uses four appropriate resources; documents sources.	Relies on only one or two sources; sources not documented.	No evidence of resources used.
Organization	Includes interesting introduction; paragraphs logically sequenced and contain subtle transitions; strong conclusion.	Contains introduction; paragraphs are adequately developed but many do not include clear transitions; conclusion is present.	Logical organization; introduction and conclusion not fully developed; transitions between paragraphs missing.	Weak organization; facts and details are stated without connections or transitions; introduction and conclusion inadequate or missing.
Creativity	Demonstrates careful thought and initiative; contains original ideas.	Evidence of some creative thought present.	Contains one or two interesting details.	No original ideas or methods evident.
Presentation	Neatly typed; pages numbered; cover sheet with name, date, and grade; graphics well drawn and attractive.	Easy to read; includes cover sheet and other required features; graphics are neatly presented.	Legible but lacking in visual appeal; missing cover sheet or another required feature; graphics somewhat messy.	Difficult to read; no cover sheet; graphics are illegible.

Rubric for Assessing a Writing Assignment

Grading Criteria	Excellent	Acceptable	Minimal	Unacceptable
Content	Clearly focused introduction; idea development interesting and sophisticated; supporting evidence detailed, accurate, and convincing; perceptive conclusion.	Introduction gives assignment direction; idea development clear; supporting evidence accurate; strong conclusion.	Introduction unclear; idea development uneven and simplistic; supporting evidence uneven; conclusion summarizes information in assignment.	Introduction incomplete, ineffective; idea development ineffective; supporting evidence vague, inaccurate, or missing; conclusion incomplete or missing.
Organization	Paragraph order reinforces content; strong topic sentences make content easy to follow; effective and varied transitions.	Logical paragraph order; clear topic sentences; clear and functional transitions.	Ineffective paragraph order; narrow or inaccurate topic sentences; few clear transitions.	Inconsistent paragraph order; topic sentences and transitions missing.
Mechanics	Flawless punctuation and spelling; varied and interesting sentence structure.	Few spelling and punctuation errors; sentence structure correct.	Some careless spelling and punctuation errors; some errors in sentence structure.	Many spelling and punctuation errors; many sentence fragments and run-ons.

Rubric for Assessing a Student Poster

Grading Criteria	Excellent	Acceptable	Minimal	Unacceptable
Content	Well-written text and carefully chosen visuals work together to illustrate and inform about poster subject.	Descriptive text and appropriate visuals work together to inform viewers.	Text contains inaccuracies, and some visual materials lack pertinence or impact.	Text sparse and inaccurate; visuals lack impact.
Design	Logical and easy to read; type and visuals neatly executed; layout complements the content.	Fairly logical; type and visuals mostly neat and easy to understand.	Somewhat disorganized; fails to complement content.	Disorganized; hastily and carelessly planned.
Visual Appeal	Pleasing use of color, shapes, symbols, and other graphic elements captures viewers' attention and interest.	Good use of color and eye-catching graphic elements.	Good ideas overshadowed by other elements that distract or give a cluttered appearance.	Little constructive use of color or graphic elements.
Creativity	Incorporates unique but pertinent ideas, design elements, visuals, or text that makes the poster stand out.	Contains some unique or imaginative elements.	Contains some good, although not entirely original elements.	No evidence of creativity.

Name _____ Class _____ Date _____

Rubric for Assessing a Letter to the Editor

Grading Criteria	Excellent	Acceptable	Minimal	Unacceptable
Idea Development	Takes a strong, well-defined position; presents appropriate reasons, supporting details, and facts.	Takes a clear position; presents some reasons and details, but does not fully develop argument.	Position not clearly stated; gives unrelated, unsupported general statements, reasons, and details; minimal facts used.	Does not take a clear position; ideas are undeveloped; no facts or details used to support position.
Organization	Contains topic sentence clearly related to position; well-developed paragraphs present ideas and details; transitions are used to enhance organization; strong conclusion evident.	Topic sentence is logical and comprehensive; paragraph order demonstrates clear plan; transitions are clear; conclusion restates position effectively.	Topic sentence blandly states position; paragraphs not ordered effectively; conclusion present but not developed.	No position or conclusion; paragraphs in no particular order; ideas not logically organized.
Mechanics and Style	Sentences interesting and varied; flawless punctuation and spelling; rich vocabulary.	Sentence construction correct and varied; a few punctuation and spelling errors; contains a few rich vocabulary words.	Sentence structure contains some variety, but is incorrect in places; careless errors in spelling and punctuation; weak use of language.	Sentences are repetitious; multiple errors in structure, spelling, and punctuation; weak and incorrect use of vocabulary.
Presentation	Neatly typed; contains date, correct addresses (return and destination), and signature.	Presented neatly, contains necessary elements.	Presented legibly; missing one or two necessary elements.	Difficult to read; lacking important elements, such as signature and return address.

Rubric for Assessing an Oral Presentation

Grading Criteria	Excellent	Acceptable	Minimal	Unacceptable
Preparation	Gathers information from varied sources; makes notecards to use as cues during the presentation; creates attractive visual aids to illustrate the presentation.	Gathers information from three or four sources; prepares notes and visual aids to use during presentation.	Gathers information from one or two sources; writes presentation word-for-word as it will be given.	Gathers information from only one source; may no be able to complete task because of lack of preparation.
Content	Abundance of material clearly related to topic; points clearly made; varied use of materials.	Adequate information about the topic; many good points made; some variation in use of materials.	Some information not connected to the topic.	Information includes little connection to topic.
Organization	Information is well organized and logically ordered; argument easy to follow; conclusion clear.	Most information presented in logical order; argument generally clear and easy to follow.	Ideas loosely connected; organization and flow choppy and somewhat difficult to follow.	No apparent logical order of information in presentation.
Speaking Skills	Enthusiastic, poised, and confident during the presentation; uses complete sentences; speaks clearly.	Engaged during presentation; speaks mostly in complete sentences.	Little or no expression; enunciation not always clear; speaks mostly in sentence fragments.	Appears disinterested during presentation; hard to understand.

Rubric for Assessing a Timeline

Grading Criteria	Excellent	Acceptable	Minimal	Unacceptable
Entry Choice	Great care taken in selection of timeline entries; most significant events, those that show historical patterns, or those that show cause-and-effect relationship selected.	Selections meet assignment criteria; few inaccuracies.	Includes required number of entries; some inaccuracies.	Does not include required number of entries.
Scale and Sequence	Scale consistent and accurate; increments marked; all entries in sequence and placed with care.	Scale accurate; increments marked; entries in sequence.	Scale roughly drawn; increments fairly accurately marked; some entries out of sequence.	No apparent scale; increments not marked; many entries out of sequence.
Mechanics	Flawless.	Few mechanical errors.	Some errors in spelling and dates.	Many errors in spelling and dates.
Visual Presentation	Visually striking; very effective in communicating historical information.	Clear and uncluttered.	Legible.	Illegible and messy.

Core Concepts Part 1
Tools of Geography

Test A

Key Terms

Complete each statement.

1. Map makers use units called _____ to measure latitude and longitude on Earth's surface.

2. Geographers use the term _____ to describe one half of Earth.

3. Images such as _____ can show certain features in greater detail than maps can.

4. Modern geographers sometimes use _____, which are computer devices that store data about locations.

5. Map makers use different types of _____ to show flat images of Earth's rounded surface.

6. Some maps include a _____ to show the broader location of the area displayed on the main map.

7. The _____ on a map shows the major directions for the area displayed on that map.

8. To find out how many U.S. states border Mexico, you would look at a _____.

9. If you say that Canada is north of the United States, you are giving a _____ for each country.

10. Geographers would define an area that shared a common climate as a single _____ in terms of its weather.

Key Ideas

Identify the choice that best completes the statement or answers the question.

_____ 11. Most maps have a key and a scale bar in order to
   a. display degrees of longitude and latitude.
   b. indicate north, south, east, and west.
   c. provide information on distance and map symbols.
   d. show the area on the map in relationship to a larger area.

_____ 12. What type of map would you use to find the elevation of mountain ranges?
   a. A physical map
   b. A political map
   c. A special-purpose map
   d. A road map

_____ 13. Which of the following is one of the five themes of geography that is useful when studying different places?
   a. Political history
   b. Economics
   c. Culture
   d. Movement

Core Concepts

Core Concepts Part 1
Tools of Geography

Test A

Critical Thinking

14. Why would you use a map instead of a globe or an aerial photograph to find your way around a city?

_____

_____

_____

_____

15. How would you find the distance, in miles, between two points on a map?

_____

_____

_____

_____

16. Describe the major physical and human features of the location where you live, such as the landscape, weather, and population. What theme of geography are you using in your description?

_____

_____

_____

_____

Essay

17. NASA wants to show the surface of the planet Mars using the same tools that geographers use to show Earth's surface. Apply your knowledge of the available types of tools and maps to describe what general kinds of Mars data they would display.

_____

_____

_____

_____

_____

_____

_____

_____

_____

_____

Core Concepts

Core Concepts Part 1
Tools of Geography

Test B

Key Terms

Complete each statement.

1. Lines of _____ measure the distance north or south of the Equator.

2. North-south lines on a globe measure _____, the distance east or west of the Prime Meridian.

3. Showing our round Earth on a flat surface leads to _____ in the shape or position of objects.

4. Modern geographers can view _____, pictures of Earth's surface taken from orbit.

5. Look at the _____ of a map to understand the meaning of that map's symbols and shading.

6. To find out how much real-world distance is represented by a given space on a map, look at the _____ of that map.

7. By looking at a _____, geographers can quickly locate and identify natural features of an area.

8. Areas of low _____ are often found close to the seashore.

9. The _____ of the Capitol Building is 38°54'N, 77°2'W.

10. The geographic theme of _____ deals with how people, goods, and ideas travel from one place to another.

Key Ideas

Identify the choice that best completes the statement or answers the question.

_____ 11. Which part of a map would you look at to find directions on a physical map?
   a. Scale bar
   b. Compass rose
   c. Locator map
   d. Key

_____ 12. What type of map would you look at to find the voting results for a recent presidential election?
   a. A political map
   b. A physical map
   c. A special-purpose map
   d. A Mercator projection map

_____ 13. When a geographer studies the migration patterns of humans over many centuries and how that has affected the geography of North America, which theme of geography is he or she using?
   a. Location
   b. Region
   c. Place
   d. Movement

Core Concepts

Core Concepts Part 1
Tools of Geography

Test B

Critical Thinking

14. What advantages does a globe have over a map or a satellite image?

_____

_____

_____

_____

15. Explain why a compass rose appears on many different types of maps.

_____

_____

_____

_____

16. Describe the location of your school in relation to a nearby building. What theme of geography are you using?

_____

_____

_____

_____

Essay

17. You have been asked to send visual information about your hometown to students in a foreign country. Describe the different geographic tools and types of maps that you could use to show your hometown. Then, choose one type of map and one other method that would best display geographic information about your community. Support your selections.

_____

_____

_____

_____

_____

_____

_____

_____

_____

_____

Core Concepts

Core Concepts Part 2
Our Planet Earth

Test A

Key Terms

Complete each statement.

1. Earth travels around the Sun along an oval-shaped path called an

_____.

2. During an _____, days and nights are nearly equal in length.

3. The world is divided into many areas that share the same time, known as

_____.

4. The continents and the ocean floor are both part of Earth's _____.

5. Water, ice, and wind are some of the forces that cause the _____
of rock and soil.

6. A flat area rising above the surrounding land is called a _____.

7. Earth's crust is made of huge _____ that move very slowly.

Key Ideas

Identify the choice that best completes the statement or answers the question.

_____ **8.** Day and night are caused by
   a. the rotation of Earth on its axis.
   b. the revolution of Earth around the sun.
   c. the orbit of the Moon around Earth.
   d. the distance from Earth to the sun.

_____ **9.** If it is noon in New York, which is Eastern Standard Time, what time is it in
   Denver, which is Mountain Standard Time?
   a. 2 P.M.
   b. 11 A.M.
   c. 10 A.M.
   d. 9 A.M.

_____ **10.** What causes volcanoes to erupt?
   a. The movement of continental plates creates pressure that pushes magma to
      Earth's surface.
   b. Continental plates rub against each other and cause vibrations in Earth's core.
   c. Moving continental plates push against each other and raise up Earth's crust.
   d. Pressure builds up at seams in Earth's crust, causing it to shake and release
      magma.

_____ **11.** One of the many ways that the process of deposition contributes to changing
   Earth's surface includes
   a. breaking down large landforms such as a plateaus.
   b. fracturing rocks when water freezes.
   c. building up a mountain range.
   d. creating beaches along the coastline.

Core Concepts Part 2
Our Planet Earth

Test A

Critical Thinking

12. How does the tilt of Earth's axis and its movement around the sun play a part in the changing of the seasons in the northern hemisphere?

_____

_____

_____

_____

13. What role does the mantle play in shaping Earth's crust?

_____

_____

_____

_____

14. Which landforms described in this lesson are formed by processes of deposition?

_____

_____

_____

_____

Essay

15. Describe the movements of the seven continents. Analyze this movement and hypothesize how the world's landmasses may look different in the future if the continents continue to move. What events might occur where continental plates push together?

_____

_____

_____

_____

_____

_____

_____

_____

_____

_____

Core Concepts

Core Concepts Part 2
Our Planet Earth

Test B

Key Terms

Complete each statement.

1. Earth rotates along its _____, an imaginary line drawn between the North and South Poles.

2. The _____ is a period during which days are longest in one hemisphere and shortest in the other.

3. The Earth's inner _____ is made of solid metal.

4. Shapes or kinds of land are called _____.

5. The process called _____ breaks rocks down into much smaller pieces.

6. The process of _____ can slowly create new landforms by piling up sand or small rocks.

7. The theory of _____ helps explain the movement of Earth's continents.

Key Ideas

Identify the choice that best completes the statement or answers the question.

____ 8. Time in the region surrounding the Prime Meridian is sometimes called
    a. Prime Time.
    b. London Mean Time.
    c. Global Standard Time.
    d. Universal Time.

____ 9. When it is daytime in New York City,
    a. it is daytime in the eastern hemisphere.
    b. it is nighttime on the opposite side of Earth.
    c. it is daytime across the United States.
    d. it is nighttime in the southern hemisphere.

____ 10. What causes earthquakes?
    a. Plates slide against one another, often at faults.
    b. Pressure builds up in the molten rock beneath Earth's crust and causes it to shake.
    c. Continental plates pull apart from each other, causing the crust to collapse.
    d. Continental plates press together and suddenly push up the crust.

____ 11. Weathering and erosion impact human settlement patterns because as these processes break down landforms and rocks into smaller pieces, they also contribute to
    a. dividing the continent into watersheds.
    b. generating volcanoes.
    c. creating beaches along the coastlines.
    d. providing soil for agriculture.

Core Concepts Part 2
Our Planet Earth

Test B

Critical Thinking

12. Why do the northern and southern hemispheres experience different seasons in the months of June and December?

_____

_____

_____

_____

13. What problems would life on Earth face if the planet had no atmosphere?

_____

_____

_____

_____

14. What landforms discussed in this lesson are shaped or formed by the process of erosion? Give an example of how one landform is shaped by this process.

_____

_____

_____

_____

Essay

15. Contrast the processes acting above the Earth's surface that build up landforms with the processes acting below the Earth's surface that also build up landforms. How do these two sets of processes compare to those that wear down Earth's landforms?

_____

_____

_____

_____

_____

_____

_____

_____

_____

_____

Core Concepts

Core Concepts Part 3
Climates and Ecosystems

Test A

Key Terms

Complete each statement.

1. The area between the Tropic of Cancer and the Arctic Circle is one of Earth's two

   _____.

3. By looking outside to decide what you will wear that day, you are checking the

   _____.

4. The three parts of the water cycle are _____, condensation, and precipitation.

5. A _____ is type of tropical cyclone that forms over the Atlantic Ocean.

6. A _____ is a park-like landscape of grasslands with scattered trees that can survive dry spells.

7. Maritime climates exist where moist winds blow _____.

Key Ideas

Identify the choice that best completes the statement or answers the question.

_____ 7. What is the primary reason that some areas of Earth are consistently warmer than other areas of Earth?
   a. Distance from the sun
   b. Tilt of Earth's axis
   c. Altitude
   d. Seasons

_____ 8. _____ act like large rivers in the Earth's oceans and help spread Earth's heat and shape climates.
   a. Ocean currents
   b. Wind patterns
   c. Temperature differences
   d. Water cycles

_____ 9. When two air masses of different temperatures or moisture content collide, one result of this air movement may be
   a. high pressure.
   b. low pressure.
   c. a new desert area.
   d. intense storms.

_____ 10. Ecosystems can change over time because of physical processes or
   a. grass or forest fires.
   b. hurricanes or tornadoes.
   c. very cold winters.
   d. human activities.

Core Concepts Part 3
Climates and Ecosystems

Critical Thinking

11. What causes temperatures in the high latitudes to be cool in the summer and bitterly cold in the winter?

_____

_____

_____

12. How does a belt of rising and sinking air form?

_____

_____

_____

13. Discuss how temperature, precipitation, and wind interact to form arid climates.

_____

_____

_____

Essay

14. Discuss the relationship between temperature, wind, and air currents, and how each affects climate types. Give examples.

_____

_____

_____

_____

_____

_____

_____

_____

Core Concepts Part 3
Climates and Ecosystems

Test B

Key Terms

Complete each statement.

1. By measuring the average day-to-day weather of a place over many years, you can describe the _____ of that place.

2. Heat from sunlight can cause water to _____ from a body of water on Earth.

3. The area of rising air near the equator is called the _____.

4. Hurricanes affect larger areas than _____, which are swirling funnels of wind.

5. The difference between deciduous trees and coniferous trees is that coniferous trees do not _____.

6. The climate types found where there is steadily sinking air are

   _____.

Key Ideas

Identify the choice that best completes the statement or answers the question.

_____ 7. What causes some areas of Earth to be warmer than other areas?
   a. Distance from the sun
   b. Tilt of Earth's axis
   c. Altitude
   d. Seasons

_____ 8. The two main ways to describe both weather and climate are
   _____ and temperature.
   a. wind speed
   b. precipitation
   c. weather pattern
   d. climate graph

_____ 9. The Canary Current and the Labrador Current move cool water from the poles to the tropics, where the cool water _____ the air near it.
   a. chills
   b. warms
   c. condenses
   d. clouds

_____ 10. _____, which move heat and moisture between different parts of the Earth, may lead to cyclones, hurricanes, and tornadoes.
   a. Convergence zones
   b. Wind and air currents
   c. Bands of rising air
   d. Bands of sinking air

Core Concepts

Core Concepts Part 3
Climates and Ecosystems

Test B

Critical Thinking

11. What are the three zones of latitude and why are some zones warmer than others?

_____

_____

_____

_____

12. What happens when warm air rises and loses its moisture? What effect does that have on the regions at edges of the tropics and near the poles?

_____

_____

_____

_____

13. Which of the three shapers of climate—temperature, precipitation, and wind—do you think is most important in the formation of arid climates?

_____

_____

_____

_____

Essay

14. Explain how temperature, wind, and water are important to the water cycle.

_____

_____

_____

_____

_____

_____

_____

_____

_____

_____

_____

Core Concepts

Core Concepts Part 4
Human-Environment Interaction

Test A

Key Terms

Complete each statement.

1. When _____ resources are used up, they are gone for good, because they cannot be replenished.

2. The ways people use land are affected by both the _____ and their culture.

3. Land uses that cover large areas include cropland, forests, and

_____.

4. Animals that live in a forest may be harmed if people bring about the

_____ of a region.

Key ideas

Identify the choice that best completes the statement or answers the question.

_____ 5. A useful material found in the environment is known as a
   a. nonrenewable resource.
   b. energy resource.
   c. natural resource.
   d. renewable resource.

_____ 6. Which of the following is an example of a nonrenewable resource?
   a. Oil
   b. Soil
   c. Water
   d. Animals

_____ 7. _____ is the movement of new settlers and their culture into a new area.
   a. Land use
   b. Colonization
   c. Industrialization
   d. Environmental change

_____ 8. Both deforestation and drilling oil wells can reduce
   a. ecosystems.
   b. biodiversity.
   c. pollution.
   d. spillover.

_____ 9. Pollution is considered a spillover because
   a. it is often caused by chemical spills.
   b. the environment can't absorb enough of the pollutants.
   c. water pollution is the most dangerous type of pollution.
   d. it affects parts of the environment not involved in the activity that caused the pollution.

Core Concepts Part 4
Human-Environment Interaction

Test A

Critical Thinking

10. Discuss the impact that colonization may have on land use.

_____

_____

_____

_____

11. Where in the United States would you most likely find much of the nation's agricultural activities?

_____

_____

_____

_____

12. What does it mean that people extract natural resources from the environment? How can extracting resources harm ecosystems and the environment?

_____

_____

_____

_____

Essay

13. How might colonization and industrialization affect renewable and nonrenewable resources?

_____

_____

_____

_____

_____

_____

_____

_____

_____

_____

_____

_____

Core Concepts

Core Concepts Part 4
Human-Environment Interaction

Test B

Key Terms

Complete each statement.

1. Humans depend on their _____ to provide food, water, energy, and other materials that are necessary for human survival.

2. Soil, plants, water, and animals are all examples of major _____ resources.

3. Technology has made it possible for people to change their environment by building _____ on the edges of cities and large towns.

4. When pollution affects someone or something not involved in the activity that produces the pollution, this effect is called a _____.

Key Ideas

Identify the choice that best completes the statement or answers the question.

_____ 5. It is unlikely that Earth will ever run out of
  a. petroleum.
  b. plants.
  c. minerals.
  d. natural gas.

_____ 6. Since the 1800s, what human activity has changed landscapes and led to the growth of large cities in many countries?
  a. Industrialization
  b. Colonization
  c. Suburbs
  d. Technology

_____ 7. Which factor is most likely to change a region's landscape?
  a. Temperature
  b. Climate
  c. Oceans
  d. Settlers

_____ 8. Some chemicals used by farmers may harm the environment by causing
  a. deforestation.
  b. oil spills.
  c. pollution.
  d. spillover.

_____ 9. A common reason for pollution is that it is produced by an activity that
  a. should never be done.
  b. has no beneficial impacts.
  c. is against the law.
  d. leads to economic growth.

Core Concepts

Core Concepts Part 4
Human-Environment Interaction

Test B

Critical Thinking

10. How have industrialization and the growth of cities changed land use in some areas of the United States?

_____

_____

_____

_____

11. What determines the way in which people use land? What are some things that can change the way in which land is used?

_____

_____

_____

_____

12. How can using resources for growing food or producing other goods and services affect the environment?

_____

_____

_____

_____

Essay

13. What is biodiversity? Do you think that biodiversity is important? Why or why not?

_____

_____

_____

_____

_____

_____

_____

_____

_____

_____

Core Concepts

Core Concepts Part 5
Economics and Geography

Test A

Key Terms

Complete each statement.

1. A(n)_____ is a factor that encourages people to make choices to act in a certain way.

2. _____ is the desire for a certain good or service.

3. _____ is the money a company has left after subtracting the costs of doing business.

4. A general increase in prices over time is called _____.

5. An economy in which the central government makes all economic decisions is a(n) _____.

6. A(n) _____ is a country with a strong economy and a high standard of living.

7. The amount of goods and services produced given the amount of resources used is called _____.

8. _____ are goods and services produced within a country and sold outside the country's borders.

9. A government policy or restriction that limits international trade is a(n) _____.

10. The price paid for borrowing money is _____.

11. A(n) _____ is a share of ownership in a company.

Key Ideas

Identify the choice that best completes the statement or answers the question.

_____ 12. Which type of economic system has the highest level of government control?
   a. Traditional economy
   b. Market economy
   c. Command economy
   d. Mixed economy

_____ 13. Which of the following are ways to increase economic development?
   a. Encouraging more farming
   b. Investing in education and training
   c. Establishing price controls
   d. Lowering wages

_____ 14. Which describes the type of buying and selling that takes place within a country?
   a. Free trade
   b. International trade
   c. Tariff
   d. Domestic trade

Core Concepts

Core Concepts Part 5
Economics and Geography

Test A

Critical Thinking

15. What happens to producers and consumers during a recession?

_____

_____

_____

_____

16. What is the role of the government in a mixed economy?

_____

_____

_____

_____

_____

17. How can technology affect a country's economic development?

_____

_____

_____

_____

Essay

18. Would people in a developed country or a developing country be more likely to invest their money? How does that affect the people's well-being?

_____

_____

_____

_____

_____

_____

_____

_____

_____

_____

Core Concepts Part 5
Economics and Geography

Test B

Key Terms

Complete each statement.

1. The amount of a good that is available for use is known as _____.

2. A(n) _____ is an organized way for producers and consumers to trade goods and services.

3. The act of concentrating on a limited number of goods or activities is known as _____.

4. Companies' profits are affected by _____, which is the struggle among producers for consumers' money.

5. A(n) _____ is an economy in which individual consumers and producers make economic decisions.

6. _____ is economic growth, or an increase in living standards.

7. _____ is the practical application of knowledge to accomplish a task.

8. _____ are goods and services sold in a country that are produced in other countries.

9. Today, many countries are working toward_____, or the removal of trade barriers.

10. _____ is an arrangement in which a buyer can borrow money to purchase something and pay for it over time.

11. _____ is the act of using money to try to make a future profit.

Key Ideas

Identify the choice that best completes the statement or answers the question.

_____ 12. Most societies have which type of economic system?
   a. Traditional economy
   b. Market economy
   c. Command economy
   d. Mixed economy

_____ 13. Compared to a developing country, a developed country is likely to have which of the following?
   a. A less-productive economy
   b. Lower standards of living
   c. A stronger economy
   d. Lower productivity

_____ 14. Which of the following is a likely result of trade barriers?
   a. Protection of domestic producers from competition
   b. Lower prices
   c. More choices
   d. Increase in imports

Core Concepts

Core Concepts Part 5
Economics and Geography

Test B

Critical Thinking

15. How can a recession lead to unemployment?

_____

_____

_____

_____

16. What is one similarity and one difference between the economies of Japan and Cuba?

_____

_____

_____

_____

17. How can improving education and training for a country's people affect the country's development?

_____

_____

_____

_____

Essay

18. What are some characteristics of a country that may influence its leaders to prefer tariffs? What are some characteristics that may cause a country's leaders to prefer free trade?

_____

_____

_____

_____

_____

_____

_____

_____

_____

_____

_____

Core Concepts

Core Concepts Part 6
Population and Movement

Test A

Key Terms

Complete each statement.

1. The _____ is the number of live births per 1,000 people in a year.

2. The number of people per square mile or other unit of land area is known as the _____ of that area.

3. Migration may be described as _____ migration, emigration, or immigration.

4. _____ attract people to new countries.

5. People in poor, overcrowded neighborhoods, called _____, often live in shacks or run-down buildings.

6. The movement of people from rural areas to urban areas is called

   _____.

7. In _____ sprawl, new, spread-out neighborhoods replace farmland and wilderness areas.

Key Ideas

Identify the choice that best completes the statement or answers the question.

_____ 8. A country's _____ is the total number of people living within its borders.
   a. population density
   b. population
   c. population growth
   d. population distribution

_____ 9. Causes of migration that push people to leave their home country are called
   a. pull factors.
   b. push factors.
   c. new customs.
   d. involuntary migrations.

_____ 10. _____ and _____ are two problems created by urbanization.
   a. More jobs; new highways
   b. Slums; suburban sprawl
   c. Education; better lives for children
   d. Better health care; new water lines

_____ 11. One cause for the rapid population growth since the time of the Industrial Revolution is
   a. better medical care.
   b. high infant mortality.
   c. food shortages.
   d. poor sanitation.

Core Concepts Part 6
Population and Movement

Test A

Critical Thinking

12. How can rapid population growth affect the infant mortality rate?

_____

_____

_____

_____

13. What are two reasons that people from all over the world emigrate to the United States?

_____

_____

_____

_____

14. What is urbanization, and how does it affect people who are long-time city residents?

_____

_____

_____

_____

Essay

15. How can demographers use a country's population distribution and population density to help governments prepare for the future?

_____

_____

_____

_____

_____

_____

_____

_____

_____

_____

Core Concepts Part 6
Population and Movement

Test B

Key Terms

Complete each statement.

1. The _____ is the number of deaths per 1,000 people in a year.

2. Unfortunately, problems caused by rapid population growth can lead to deaths of many infants, giving an area a high _____.

3. How people are spread out over an area of land is that area's _____.

4. A newcomer who arrives from elsewhere and settles in a new country is called a(n) _____.

5. Cities with high population densities tend to have crowded roads and crowded _____.

6. _____ migrations have generally involved the forced movement of enslaved people.

7. One of the challenges of urban growth is suburban _____.

Key Ideas

Identify the choice that best completes the statement or answers the question.

_____ 8. A tool used to describe how thickly or thinly an area is settled is called
   a. population density.
   b. total population.
   c. population growth.
   d. population distribution.

_____ 9. A _____ is one example of a pull factor.
   a. flood
   b. famine
   c. war
   d. supply of good jobs

_____ 10. People who live in poor, overcrowded urban areas, or _____, are unable to meet their basic needs.
   a. urban areas
   b. slums
   c. rural areas
   d. suburbs

_____ 11. Rapid population growth can result in large increases in the infant morality rate if there is
   a. a shortage of food and clean water.
   b. a higher consumption of goods and services.
   c. an industrial plant located nearby.
   d. an extended period of migration.

Core Concepts Part 6
Population and Movement

Test B

Critical Thinking

12. How can population growth affect the environment?

_____

_____

_____

_____

13. How is it possible for the total population of a country to grow even when the country's population growth rate is very small?

_____

_____

_____

_____

_____

14. How might spreading suburbs affect the lives of the people who are living on the farmland and in the open spaces?

_____

_____

_____

_____

Essay

15. How can migration change a country's plans for population growth, distribution, and density? What impact can migration have on planning?

_____

_____

_____

_____

_____

_____

_____

_____

_____

_____

_____

Core Concepts Part 7
Culture and Geography

Test A

Key Terms

Complete each statement.

1. Human activities create geographic areas that have been shaped by people, which are also called _____.

2. A pattern of organized relationships among groups of people within a society is a(n)

   _____.

3. A family that includes parents, children, grandparents, aunts, uncles, and other family members is a(n) _____ family.

4. People who speak different languages sometimes turn to a(n)

   _____ in order to communicate with each other.

5. Religion can help guide people in standards of acceptable behavior, or

   _____.

6. Settlement, trade, migration, and communication are among the ways that

   _____ takes place.

Key Ideas

Identify the choice that best completes the statement or answers the question.

_____ 7. A group of humans with a shared culture who have organized themselves to meet their basic needs is a(n)
   a. family.
   b. society.
   c. social structure.
   d. extended family.

_____ 8. In a society, architectural works can be important _____ symbols.
   a. government
   b. cultural
   c. geographical
   d. resource

_____ 9. Cultures often develop along with science and
   a. tools.
   b. technology.
   c. agriculture.
   d. machines.

_____ 10. An area in which a single culture or cultural trait is dominant is called a
   a. culture.
   b. cultural landscape.
   c. norm.
   d. culture region.

Core Concepts

Core Concepts Part 7
Culture and Geography

Test A

Critical Thinking

11. Do political boundaries always match the boundaries of culture regions? Explain your reasoning.

_____

_____

_____

_____

12. How do cultures change?

_____

_____

_____

_____

13. Why was refrigeration such an important technological development?

_____

_____

_____

_____

Essay

14. Do you think that some cultures change faster than others? Why or why not? Explain your reasoning.

_____

_____

_____

_____

_____

_____

_____

_____

_____

_____

_____

_____

Core Concepts Part 7
Culture and Geography

Test B

Key Terms

Complete each statement.

1. A behavior that is considered normal in a particular society is a(n)

   _____.

2. A(n) _____ family is one consisting of parents and their children.

3. The world has about 12 major language groups. Languages within each of these groups share a common _____.

4. Ramadan, a time to avoid food during daytime, to pray, and to read the Quran, is a holy month for _____.

5. The thousands of distinct religious traditions that tend to be passed down by word of mouth instead of through sacred text are called _____.

6. When customs and ideas are spread by settlement, trade, migration, and communication from one culture to another, _____ is taking place.

Key Ideas

Identify the choice that best completes the statement or answers the question.

_____ 7. Industrial societies often organize members according to their
   a. social structure.
   b. families.
   c. agriculture.
   d. social class.

_____ 8. Love, death, peace, and war are examples of _____ that relate to the entire world.
   a. paintings
   b. music
   c. books
   d. universal themes

_____ 9. Some people worry that rapid communication is creating a new global culture that threatens
   a. migration.
   b. cultural hearths.
   c. diversity.
   d. communication.

_____ 10. The basis for culture is
   a. language.
   b. sounds.
   c. symbols.
   d. gestures.

Core Concepts

Core Concepts Part 7
Culture and Geography

Test B

Critical Thinking

11. Why are parts of southwest Asia and northern Africa joined in a single culture region?

_____

_____

_____

12. What do you think is the reason that it usually takes time for a culture to change?

_____

_____

_____

_____

13. How is a Sumerian chariot from about 5,000 years ago different from a convertible automobile from the 1950s? How are the two vehicles similar?

_____

_____

_____

_____

Essay

14. Why are language and religion so important to culture and society?

_____

_____

_____

_____

_____

_____

_____

_____

_____

_____

_____

Core Concepts

Core Concepts Part 8
Government and Citizenship

Test A

Key Terms

Complete each statement.

1. Most modern governments have a(n) _____ that outlines the rules and principles of their organization.

2. The leaders of the government have the power to make all decisions for the country in a(n) _____ government.

3. All laws are passed by the central government under a(n) _____.

4. Countries create _____ to describe how they plan to interact with the governments of other countries.

5. If two or more countries have a conflict, they may sign a(n) _____ to help resolve it.

6. Voting is one example of taking part in government, also called _____.

Key Ideas

Identify the choice that best completes the statement or answers the question.

_____ 7. A state containing several countries is called
   a. an empire.
   b. a monarchy.
   c. a democracy.
   d. communist.

_____ 8. The principle of majority rule means that the U.S. government
   a. can pass any law without worrying about minority rights.
   b. can only pass laws voted for by a majority of representatives.
   c. is bound by the rule of law.
   d. must have the support of a majority of local governments for the action of the regional government.

_____ 9. Which of the following statements is most accurate?
   a. In the past, there were many democracies that protected the rights of citizens.
   b. The rise of democracies that protect citizens' rights is a fairly recent event in world history.
   c. There are very few democratic governments in the world today.
   d. Most democracies fail to protect the rights of their citizens.

_____ 10. Which of the following is an example of something that a limited government would do, but is probably something that an unlimited government would not be willing to do?
   a. Build and maintain public roads
   b. Protect citizens from attack
   c. Operate public schools
   d. Let citizens speak freely in public

Core Concepts

Core Concepts Part 8
Government and Citizenship

Test A

Critical Thinking

11. Compare and contrast the governments of ancient Athens and the United States.

_____

_____

_____

_____

12. Compare the legislative, executive, and judicial branches of the U.S. government. Consider the highest office or institution in each branch; the role of each branch in making, enforcing, or interpreting laws; and any other powers each branch has. Compare and contrast the governments of ancient Athens and the United States.

_____

_____

_____

_____

13. What role does the United Nations play in global diplomacy and human rights?

_____

_____

_____

_____

Essay

14. Why might a nation cooperate with some countries and come into conflict with others? Do you think that the types of governments that two countries have can make them more or less likely to cooperate with each other? Explain.

_____

_____

_____

_____

_____

_____

_____

Core Concepts Part 8
Government and Citizenship

Test B

Key Terms

Complete each statement.

1. Laws restrict the powers of a(n) _____ government.

2. The unjust use of power is known as _____.

3. The United States has a(n) _____, in which power is divided between different levels of government.

4. Most governments use _____ to manage their relationships with each other in a peaceful way.

5. _____ includes all those activities that have to do with a person's society and community.

6. Members of a(n) _____ try to influence public policy on specific issues.

Key Ideas

Identify the choice that best completes the statement or answers the question.

_____ 7. Which form of government has a king or queen that shares powers with the people of the state and the other branches of government?
    a. Absolute monarchy
    b. Constitutional monarchy
    c. Representative democracy
    d. Authoritarian communism

_____ 8. The principle of giving each branch of government the power to cancel the action of another branch is called
    a. separation of powers.
    b. checks and balances.
    c. the federal system.
    d. minority rights.

_____ 9. Which of the following statements best describes human rights in the world today?
    a. All people around the world are part of a global community, so everyone enjoys the same rights.
    b. Democracies are most likely to protect human rights of their citizens.
    c. There is less support for human rights around the world today than there was in the past.
    d. Non-democratic governments usually protect the basic rights of their citizens

_____ 10. Which of the following international organizations works to prevent and solve economic crises around the world?
    a. United Nations
    b. Amnesty International
    c. World Bank
    d. International Monetary Fund

Core Concepts

Core Concepts Part 8
Government and Citizenship

Critical Thinking

11. Compare and contrast limited and unlimited governments.

_____

_____

_____

_____

12. Compare and contrast states and nation-states.

_____

_____

_____

_____

13. In what ways do governments and international organizations try to address the harmful effects of conflict?

_____

_____

_____

_____

Essay

14. Would you have the same rights and responsibilities if you were a citizen of another country? What are the sorts of things that might contribute to your rights being the same or different in another country?

_____

_____

_____

_____

_____

_____

_____

_____

_____

_____

Core Concepts Part 9
Tools of History

Test A

Key Terms

Complete each statement.

1. A _____ is a line marked off with a series of events and dates.

2. The time before humans invented writing is called _____.

3. A(n) _____ is information that comes directly from a person who experienced an event.

4. An encyclopedia article describing a historical event that took place 250 years ago is an example of a _____ source.

5. The study of humankind in all aspects, especially development and culture, is _____.

6. A person who explores places where people once lived, searching for artifacts to learn about the past, is practicing _____.

7. A(n) _____ would be a good source to use if you wanted to understand how landforms like rivers and hills affected a battle.

Key Ideas

Identify the choice that best completes the statement or answers the question.

_____ 8. Which of the following is a list of events, organized in the order in which they occurred?
   a. Period
   b. Chronology
   c. Era
   d. Epoch

_____ 9. What type of information can be shown best on a historical map?
   a. Migration
   b. Weather
   c. Political boundaries
   d. Population

_____ 10. What element of a historical map is most likely to tell you what period of time the map shows?
   a. Locator map
   b. Key
   c. Title
   d. Shape

_____ 11. Which of the following is true for historians evaluating the reliability of primary sources?
   a. Because the source witnessed the events, a historian can trust it completely.
   b. Only sources provided by college professors are considered reliable.
   c. Sources must be compared to articles from the Internet.
   d. A historian must look for evidence of bias.

Core Concepts

Core Concepts Part 9
Tools of History

Test A

Critical Thinking

12. Which of these types of primary sources—letters, diary entries, speeches, artifacts—would be least likely to show bias? Explain your answer.

_____

_____

_____

13. Why do historians study primary sources?

_____

_____

_____

_____

14. Why might some ancient cultures have had strong oral traditions?

_____

_____

_____

Essay

15. If you wanted to research a topic in history, would a primary source or a secondary source be more valuable? Explain your answer.

_____

_____

_____

_____

_____

_____

_____

_____

_____

_____

Core Concepts Part 9
Tools of History

Test B

Key Terms
Complete each statement.

1. A person who studies events that took place during the past is a

   _____.

2. A list of events in the order in which they occurred is called a

   _____.

3. A(n) _____ is information about an event that does not come from a person who experienced that event.

4. An example of a _____ source is photograph taken on the day of a historic event.

5. A(n) _____ is an unfair preference for or dislike of something or someone.

6. The scientific study of ancient cultures through the examination of artifacts and other evidence is called _____.

7. Someone who studies _____ seeks to understand the origin of humans and how humans developed physically.

Key Ideas
Identify the choice that best completes the statement or answers the question.

_____ 8. A song about a hunt may form an important part of a society's
   a. artifacts.
   b. archaeology.
   c. anthropology.
   d. oral tradition.

_____ 9. Why is a historical map a good type of map to use to study trade patterns?
   a. A historical map shows place names.
   b. A historical map can show movement over time.
   c. A historical map has a compass rose.
   d. A historical map has a key.

_____ 10. What type of information do historical maps offer?
   a. Primary
   b. Archaeological
   c. Oral
   d. Visual

_____ 11. Which of the following is a reason why historians may want to consider a source's opinions as well as the facts reported by a source?
   a. A source that a historian trusts is likely to have true opinions.
   b. The opinions may provide clues to the source's feelings and possible bias.
   c. Examining opinions will reveal whether it is a primary or secondary source.
   d. The opinions will reveal the identity of the source.

Core Concepts

Core Concepts Part 9
Tools of History

Test B

Critical Thinking

12. What are two situations that may cause a primary source to be an unreliable account of what actually happened?

_____

_____

_____

_____

13. What might an artifact tell a historian about a society in the past?

_____

_____

_____

_____

14. What kinds of information might a historian learn from a community's oral tradition?

_____

_____

_____

_____

Essay

15. What type of historical information would a historical map show less effectively than another type of source would?

_____

_____

_____

_____

_____

_____

_____

_____

_____

Core Concepts

CHAPTER

1

The United States

Test A

Key Terms

Complete each statement.

1. In general, the continental United States has a _____ climate.

2. Agricultural goods are the main _____ of the United States to other nations around the world.

Key Ideas

Identify the choice that best completes the statement or answers the question.

_____ 3. The highest elevations in the United States are located in
   a. the Sierra Nevada.
   b. the Great Plains.
   c. the Rocky Mountains.
   d. the coastal regions.

_____ 4. Which of the following doubled the size of the United States in 1803?
   a. The Civil War
   b. The Louisiana Purchase
   c. The American Revolution
   d. The Industrial Revolution

_____ 5. The Native American living in the _____ were most likely to use canoes.
   a. Eastern woodlands
   b. Great Basin
   c. Plains
   d. Southwest

_____ 6. Many immigrants were likely drawn to the United States because of the individual rights and freedoms guaranteed by the
   a. Constitution.
   b. doctrine of Manifest Destiny.
   c. civil rights movement.
   d. Industrial Revolution.

_____ 7. NAFTA is a trade agreement among
   a. the United States, China, and India.
   b. the United States, Canada, and Mexico.
   c. the United States, Japan, and Mexico.
   d. the United States, South America, and the Middle East.

_____ 8. The cultural diversity of the United States tends to be highest
   a. in the Midwest and central states.
   b. along the border with Canada.
   c. along the border with Mexico.
   d. in New England.

Chapter Tests

CHAPTER

1 **The United States**   **Test A**

Critical Thinking

9. How might natural features help explain the lower population density of the western states?

_____

_____

_____

_____

10. How did the idea of Manifest Destiny affect Native Americans?

_____

_____

_____

_____

_____

11. Why is diplomacy a key part of U.S. foreign policy?

_____

_____

_____

_____

Essay

12. Discuss the importance of immigration in shaping the United States. Give at least one example each of how immigration has influenced the nation's economy, culture, and population.

_____

_____

_____

_____

_____

_____

_____

_____

_____

_____

_____

_____

_____

Chapter Tests

1 The United States   Test B

Key Terms

Complete each statement.

1. The United States has experienced a steady shift in population from the countryside to cities and _____, or areas in which several cities are geographically close together.

2. The United States has a _____, in which decisions on what to buy or sell are made by individuals and businesses, rather than by a centralized government or other authority.

Key Ideas

Identify the choice that best completes the statement or answers the question.

_____ 3. Which of the following physical features attracted settlers who were looking for easier ways to travel?
   a. Rivers   **c.** The Great Lakes
   b. Mountains   **d.** The Great Plains

_____ 4. Which of the following statements about the natural resources of the United States is most accurate?
   a. The many agricultural resources of the United States have made up for its lack of other resources.
   b. U.S. industry and agriculture have prospered because America has many different natural resources.
   c. The United States has had to import most of its resources from other nations elsewhere in the world.
   d. Natural resources such as clothing and cars have helped the U.S. economy.

_____ 5. Many Italian and Polish immigrants came to the United States
   a. before the Civil War.   **c.** in the late 1900s.
   b. in the early 1900s.   **d.** since the 1960s.

_____ 6. Native American cultures were disrupted when the Europeans arrived and introduced
   a. the idea of farming.   **c.** fishing practices.
   b. unfamiliar diseases.   **d.** dissenters.

_____ 7. The forests of the Pacific Northwest are just one of the many different _____ in the United States where many people work in the same industry.
   a. elevation regions   **c.** climate regions
   b. political regions   **d.** economic regions

_____ 8. The organization known as USAID
   a. promotes free trade.   **c.** provides food aid.
   b. provides military aid.   **d.** negotiates peace treaties.

CHAPTER

The United States

Test B

Critical Thinking

9. Compare and contrast the Appalachian Mountains and the Rocky Mountains.

_____

_____

_____

_____

10. In what ways was the civil rights movement a major change for African Americans?

_____

_____

_____

_____

11. Why might an immigrant want to become a U.S. citizen?

_____

_____

_____

_____

Essay

12. How has the cultural diversity of the United States changed over time? How is this change reflected in modern American society?

_____

_____

_____

_____

_____

_____

_____

_____

_____

_____

_____

_____

_____

Chapter Tests

CHAPTER

2 Canada

Test A

Key Terms

Complete each statement.

1. The harsh _____ climate of Northern Canada has limited the population in the region.

2. The islands of the Arctic Archipelago contain _____, soil that remains frozen even when the summer warmth temporarily melts the snow and ice that usually covers the area.

3. The colony of _____ existed alongside British Canada for many years.

4. Modern Canada is a diverse society best described as a _____ of many people who keep their own cultural identities.

Key Ideas

Identify the choice that best completes the statement or answers the question.

_____ 5. Where is the majority of Canada's oil found?
  a. Along the Atlantic Coast
  b. Along the border with the United States
  c. In western Canada
  d. Near the Arctic Ocean

_____ 6. Where is Canada's population density highest?
  a. In the cities of Northern Canada
  b. In cities in central Canada
  c. In cities along the United States border
  d. In cities along the Atlantic and Pacific Coasts

_____ 7. What natural resource most attracted European traders to Canada?
  a. Timber
  b. Animal furs
  c. Fish
  d. Whales

_____ 8. Which of the following officials has the greatest amount of executive power in the Canadian government?
  a. Prime Minister
  b. Governor General
  c. Sovereign
  d. Supreme Court

_____ 9. Canada currently ranks first in the world in which category?
  a. Total number of Internet users
  b. Percentage of college and university graduates
  c. Literacy rate of adult population
  d. Average unemployment among citizens

Chapter Tests

CHAPTER

2 Canada

Test A

Critical Thinking

10. How are Canada's settlement patterns similar to those of the United States?

_____

_____

_____

_____

11. How did Canada's growth affect its government and its ties to Great Britain?

_____

_____

_____

_____

12. If Canada had a less skilled workforce, what advantages would its economy still possess?

_____

_____

_____

Essay

13. Did Britain's actions after the Seven Years' War help or hurt cooperation between Canada's different ethnic groups? Explain your answer, then tell how Canadian law addresses multiculturalism today.

_____

_____

_____

_____

_____

_____

_____

_____

_____

_____

_____

Chapter Tests

CHAPTER

2 Canada   Test B

Key Terms

Complete each statement.

1. Canada's fishing industry benefits from the _____ where warm and cold waters combine in the Grand Banks.

2. The many lakes of the Canadian Shield region were created by _____, thick sheets of ice made of compacted snow.

3. In 1867, Canada became a _____ that governed itself but had its foreign affairs controlled by Great Britain.

4. The modern Canadian government is a _____ modeled on the government of Great Britain.

Key Ideas

Identify the choice that best completes the statement or answers the question.

____ 5. Most of Canada's border with the United States falls into which of Canada's six main climate regions?
   a. Semi-arid
   b. Maritime
   c. Continental warm summer
   d. Subarctic

____ 6. The people who first made use of the abundant resources of southern Canada were members of
   a. the First Nations.
   b. New France.
   c. British Canada.
   d. the Inuit.

____ 7. Britain guaranteed the rights of French Canadians in the
   a. Quebec Act of 1775.
   b. Act of Union.
   c. British North American Act.
   d. Dominion of Canada.

____ 8. Canada's most important trading partner is
   a. the United States.
   b. Mexico.
   c. the World Trade Organization.
   d. NATO.

____ 9. Canada has a bilingual government, which means
   a. every citizen is required to speak two languages.
   b. the country has two official languages, English and French.
   c. the country has two official languages, English and Spanish.
   d. all elected officials must be fluent in both English and French.

CHAPTER

2 **Canada** Test B

Critical Thinking

10. Give two reasons why a majority of Canadians live in cities.

_____
_____
_____
_____

11. Compare and contrast the Dominion of Canada with the Canadian government after 1931.

_____
_____
_____
_____

12. How does international trade affect Canada's economy?

_____
_____
_____
_____

Essay

13. In what ways does cultural diversity benefit Canada? In what ways does this diversity pose a political and social challenge for Canada?

_____
_____
_____
_____
_____
_____
_____
_____
_____
_____
_____

CHAPTER

3 Mexico

Test A

Key Terms

Complete each statement.

1. Differences in _____, or height above sea level, help to give Mexico a wide variety of climates.

2. The Aztecs supplied large cities with water by building _____, connecting the cities with sources of water in outlying areas.

3. The _____ began in 1910 and led to political and social reforms.

4. Mexico's economy began to grow after its leaders turned to _____ ideas.

Key Ideas

Identify the choice that best completes the statement or answers the question.

_____ 5. Compared to southern Mexico, northern Mexico
   a. has a drier climate with less yearly rainfall.
   b. has fewer temperature changes during the year.
   c. suffers from more hurricanes during the summer and fall.
   d. has a higher population.

_____ 6. Mexico's most important natural resource is
   a. gold.
   b. petroleum.
   c. coffee.
   d. corn.

_____ 7. Mexico City was built by the
   a. Olmecs, when they began to grow maize.
   b. Mayans, after they conquered the Valley of Mexico.
   c. Spanish, on the ruins of the Aztec capital.
   d. Mexican government, after Mexico gained independence.

_____ 8. How is Mexico's constitution different from the constitution of the United States?
   a. Mexico does not allow multiple political parties.
   b. Voters must be at least 21 years old.
   c. Eligible voters are required by law to vote in elections.
   d. Mexico has more than three branches of government.

_____ 9. Which of the following best describes Mexico's economy?
   a. Mexico's economy depends mainly on oil production.
   b. The government tightly controls the Mexican economy.
   c. Mexico has one of the most productive economies in the world.
   d. Mexican workers earn the same as their American and Canadian counterparts.

Chapter Tests

CHAPTER

Mexico

Test A

Critical Thinking

10. Where is most of Mexico's oil found, and why is this resource important to the country?

_____
_____
_____
_____

11. What were the short-term and long-term causes of the Mexican Revolution?

_____
_____
_____
_____

12. What encourages Mexican workers to come to the United States and how do these workers affect Mexico's economy?

_____
_____
_____
_____

Essay

13. Compare the governments of the United States and Mexico. How has Mexico's political history differed from that of the United States?

_____
_____
_____
_____
_____
_____
_____
_____
_____
_____
_____

Chapter Tests

CHAPTER

3 Mexico

Test B

Completion

Complete each statement.

1. Much of Mexico has a dry climate that farmers must _____ to help feed its growing population.

2. Hernan Cortés, who defeated the Aztec empire for the Spanish, was a _____, or soldier-explorer.

3. The PRI, or _____, ruled Mexico for most of the 1900s.

4. Many Mexicans work in the United States and send _____ back to Mexico to help support their families.

Key Ideas

Identify the choice that best completes the statement or answers the question.

_____ 5. Sinkholes are found in the
   a. Mexican Plateau.
   b. Pacific Coastal Lowlands.
   c. Sierra Madres.
   d. Yucatan Peninsula.

_____ 6. The first Native American civilization to arise in Mexico was the
   a. Olmec.
   b. Maya.
   c. Aztec.
   d. Yucatan.

_____ 7. When did Mexico gain its independence from Spain?
   a. 1810
   b. 1821
   c. 1910
   d. 1917

_____ 8. Which of the following statements best describes Mexican history?
   a. After Mexico gained independence, all land was taken from the wealthy and given to the poor.
   b. The Mexican people benefited greatly from foreign companies doing work in Mexico.
   c. After the Mexican Revolution, there were many reforms that helped the poor.
   d. Power and wealth remained in the hands of a small group, while many people remained poor.

_____ 9. Most Mexican workers are employed in
   a. farming.
   b. manufacturing jobs.
   c. service industries.
   d. the oil industry.

Chapter Tests

CHAPTER

3 Mexico

Test B

Critical Thinking

10. How is Baja California similar to and different from the rest of Mexico?

_____
_____
_____
_____

11. How do the resources of Mexico's mountains and plateaus contribute to its economy?

_____
_____
_____
_____

12. How has Mexico's government changed in recent years?

_____
_____
_____
_____

Essay

13. Was Mexico's economy stronger or weaker when it depended mainly upon its natural resources? Explain your answer, describing Mexico's key natural resources and how its economy has changed today.

_____
_____
_____
_____
_____
_____
_____
_____
_____

CHAPTER

4 Caribbean and Central America

Test A

Key Terms

Complete each statement.

1. _____ is the business of providing food, places to stay, and other services to visitors from other places.

2. Ranching and farming led to _____, or the removal of a large number of trees from an area.

3. Around 1000 B.C., Native Americans known as the _____ began settling in what is now Guatemala.

4. _____ combines Catholic and West African beliefs.

5. An increase in _____, or tourism that focuses on the environment, has led to more people exploring the region on foot or on horseback.

Key Ideas

Identify the choice that best completes the statement or answers the question.

_____ 6. A tropical climate is key to which economic activity in the lowlands of Central America and the Caribbean?
   a. Commerce and manufacturing
   b. Production of cash crops, such as sugar and coffee
   c. Livestock raising
   d. Mining

_____ 7. The group of Native Americans who settled what is now Guatemala were
   a. the Creoles.
   b. the Aztecs.
   c. the Olmecs.
   d. the Maya.

_____ 8. Sugar, African slaves, rum, tobacco, and molasses formed a triangular system of trade connecting the Caribbean with
   a. Europe and Africa.
   b. Europe and Central America.
   c. Central America and Africa.
   d. Africa and South America.

_____ 9. Foreigners continued to have influence after independence because they
   a. maintained military bases within each country.
   b. provided the investment to help build the countries' economies.
   c. advised the presidents of the new countries.
   d. controlled trade through the colonial system.

_____ 10. Most governments in Central America are
   a. dictatorships.
   b. parliamentary democracies.
   c. presidential democracies.
   d. free trade associations.

Chapter Tests

Caribbean and Central America

Test A

Critical Thinking

11. What was the encomienda system?

_____

_____

_____

_____

12. What is one cause of the diaspora of Central American and Caribbean people?

_____

_____

_____

_____

_____

13. How is ecotourism different from traditional tourism?

_____

_____

_____

_____

Essay

14. Did independence in Central America and the Caribbean bring real change to the region or not? Explain your answer.

_____

_____

_____

_____

_____

_____

_____

_____

_____

_____

CHAPTER 4 Caribbean and Central America

Test B

Key Terms

Complete each statement.

1. Caribbean islands have great _____, a wide variety of living things.

2. In Spanish colonies, the _____ system was established, which controlled the Native American population in the Spanish colonies.

3. A government controlled by a single leader is a _____.

4. Poor farmers can sometimes get small loans called _____ to start their own farms.

5. _____ is a religious festival in late winter and is primarily observed by Roman Catholics.

Key Ideas

Identify the choice that best completes the statement or answers the question.

_____ 6. Tourism is popular in Central America and the Caribbean largely because of the region's
   a. hurricanes.
   b. dry, cool highland climate.
   c. earthquakes.
   d. tropical climate.

_____ 7. Before the arrival of the Europeans, the Caribbean islands were settled by
   a. the Aztec and the Olmec.
   b. the Arawak and the Carib.
   c. the Creole and the Maya.
   d. conquistadors.

_____ 8. How did European colonists in Central America and the Caribbean deal with the huge amounts of land and labor required to grow cash crops?
   a. They imported Native Americans.
   b. They exported other crops that did not require so much land and labor.
   c. They exported enslaved Africans.
   d. They imported enslaved Africans.

_____ 9. Which country has the region's most stable democracy?
   a. Guatemala
   b. Costa Rica
   c. Haiti
   d. Dominican Republic

_____ 10. Which is a language that combines French and African influences?
   a. Creole
   b. Spanish
   c. Achi
   d. Quechua

Chapter Tests

CHAPTER

4 Caribbean and Central America

Test B

Critical Thinking

11. Why might people have different viewpoints on whether tourism is good or bad for Central America and the Caribbean?

_____

_____

_____

12. How might people in the newly independent countries of Central America and the Caribbean have disagreed over the influence of foreign powers in their countries?

_____

_____

_____

13. What are two effects of the diaspora of Central American and Caribbean people?

_____

_____

_____

Essay

14. What were the effects of colonization on Central America and the Caribbean?

_____

_____

_____

_____

_____

_____

_____

_____

_____

_____

_____

Chapter Tests

CHAPTER 5 — Caribbean South America

Test A

Key Terms

Complete each statement.

1. The three parallel ranges of the Andes Mountains in Columbia are known as

    _____.

2. After independence, _____, or dictators, soon emerged to control the governments.

3. In 1989 the government of Venezuela introduced _____, or policies meant to save money, to try to bring an end to economic decline.

4. Venezuela suffers from land _____, or the sinking of the ground, caused by decades of draining the underground oilfields.

5. In Colombia, the government has been fighting a civil war against

    _____, or rebels, for decades.

6. When the Venezuelan government took control of the country's oil industry in 1976, it _____ that industry.

Key Ideas

Identify the choice that best completes the statement or answers the question.

_____ 7. What natural resource is concentrated around Lake Maracaibo in Venezuela?
   a. Natural gas
   b. Silver
   c. Oil
   d. Gold

_____ 8. In Guyana and Suriname, the dominant ethnic group is made up of people descended from workers who migrated from
   a. India.
   b. China.
   c. Africa.
   d. France.

_____ 9. In Caribbean South America, which countries are most influenced by Spanish culture?
   a. Colombia and Venezuela
   b. Guyana, Suriname, and French Guiana
   c. Colombia and Guyana
   d. Suriname and Venezuela

_____ 10. In Suriname, the most common languages spoken are
   a. Italian and Greek.
   b. English, Dutch, and Surinamese.
   c. French, Spanish, and Surinamese.
   d. Spanish, Portuguese, and Surinamese.

Chapter Tests

CHAPTER

5 Caribbean South America

Test A

Critical Thinking

11. What were two ways in which European colonists changed the physical geography of Caribbean South America?

_____
_____
_____
_____

12. How do landforms influence where different kinds of people live in the Andes and the Pampas?

_____
_____
_____
_____

13. What effect has oil had on Venezuela's economy?

_____
_____
_____
_____

Essay

14. How well does the term "Latin America" describe the region of Caribbean South America? Explain your answer.

_____
_____
_____
_____
_____
_____
_____
_____
_____
_____
_____
_____

Chapter Tests

CHAPTER

5 Caribbean South America

Test B

Key Terms

Complete each statement.

1. The plants and animals that depend on each other and their environment for survival is called a(n) _____.

2. Sculpting a hillside into different flat areas suitable for growing crops is known as _____.

3. The Spanish hunted for treasure and a legendary gold-rich king called _____ in Caribbean South America.

4. Armed forces that are unauthorized by the government are called _____.

5. The form of democracy in which the people elect representatives to make the nation's laws is called _____.

6. The parts of the American continents that have been heavily influenced by the cultures of Spain, France, and Portugal are called _____.

Key Ideas

Identify the choice that best completes the statement or answers the question.

_____ 7. Most of Colombia's people live
   a. along the coast.
   b. in the mountains.
   c. in the east.
   d. on the border with Venezuela.

_____ 8. Who liberated the lands that later became the countries of Colombia and Venezuela?
   a. The *caudillos*
   b. Simón Bolívar
   c. The peninsulares
   d. Carlos Andrés Pérez

_____ 9. After liberation from Spain, the new countries of South America were ruled primarily by
   a. freed slaves.
   b. a small minority from the upper classes.
   c. indigenous peoples.
   d. the British.

_____ 10. In which country is the main language English?
   a. Colombia
   b. Venezuela
   c. Guyana
   d. Suriname

Chapter Tests

CHAPTER

5 Caribbean South America

Test B

Critical Thinking

11. What makes the highlands of the Andes a good place to grow many types of crops?

_____

_____

_____

12. Why might some people in colonial Caribbean South America have fought against Simón Bolívar?

_____

_____

_____

13. How might Guyana benefit from offshore oil in the future?

_____

_____

_____

Essay

14. How has the geography of Caribbean South America affected settlement and population in the region over time?

_____

_____

_____

_____

_____

_____

_____

_____

_____

_____

_____

CHAPTER 6 — The Andes and the Pampas

Test A

Key Terms

Complete each statement.

1. Mountain ranges such as the Andes are formed when one tectonic plate is _____, or pulled underneath another.

2. _____ is a regular weather event that can cause heavy rain in the Andes and Pampas.

3. So many Incans died from disease because they lacked _____.

4. After Argentina won independence, a(n) _____ was formed to govern the country.

5. Both crops and corporations help Peru to have a more _____.

Key Ideas

Identify the choice that best completes the statement or answers the question.

_____ 6. In a vertical climate zone, where would you find the coldest, wettest climate?
   a. At the lowest point
   b. At the highest point
   c. In the middle
   d. There are no cold, wet climates in a vertical climate zone.

_____ 7. The Altiplano is a high, flat area in the Andes filled with
   a. natural resources.
   b. crops.
   c. vertical climate zones.
   d. people.

_____ 8. One of the Europeans' strongest weapons against the Incas was
   a. surprise attacks.
   b. trained soldiers.
   c. disease.
   d. horses.

_____ 9. At the top of the class system during Spanish colonial times were those born in Spain, who were known as
   a. criollos.
   b. peninsulares.
   c. mestizos.
   d. gauchos.

_____ 10. An important tool used to strengthen the democracies of the Andes and Pampas is
   a. literacy.
   b. corruption.
   c. referendum.
   d. environmental policies.

CHAPTER

The Andes and the Pampas

Test A

Critical Thinking

11. Why is Buenos Aires different from other parts in the region in terms of population density?

_____

_____

_____

_____

12. Following independence, how were events in Chile and Argentina similar?

_____

_____

_____

_____

13. What is the link between European influence and cultural diversity in the Andes and the Pampas?

_____

_____

_____

_____

Essay

14. Predict how ethnic diversity in the region will continue to influence the governments of different countries.

_____

_____

_____

_____

_____

_____

_____

_____

_____

_____

_____

Chapter Tests

CHAPTER 6 The Andes and the Pampas

Test B

Key Terms

Complete each statement.

1. Farmers make use of _____ to grow different crops at different heights in the Andes.

2. An area in the Andes that is rich in silver and tin is the _____.

3. _____ were people who had European fathers and indigenous mothers.

4. The system called _____ made colonies dependent on Spain.

5. _____ is a country whose president is a Native American who champions social movements.

Key Ideas

Identify the choice that best completes the statement or answers the question.

_____ 6. What phenomenon influences the climate of the Andes and the Pampas every few years?
   a. Vertical climate zones
   b. Cordilleras
   c. Human activity
   d. El Niño

_____ 7. The Andes and the Pampas have a wide range of ecosystems because of
   a. desertification.
   b. deforestation.
   c. the effects of altitude.
   d. globalization.

_____ 8. Which empire was the largest in the Americas in the 1400s?
   a. The Pampas
   b. The Incas
   c. The Peninsulares
   d. The Mestizos

_____ 9. In the 1970s, political unrest that began with the overthrow of President Allende occurred in the country of
   a. Chile.
   b. Uruguay.
   c. Argentina.
   d. Paraguay.

_____ 10. _____ is both good and bad for the countries in the Andes and the Pampas.
   a. Literacy
   b. Deforestation
   c. Referendum
   d. Globalization

Chapter Tests

CHAPTER

6

The Andes and
the Pampas

Test B

Critical Thinking

11. What are the two largest groups of people who live in the Andes and Pampas?

_____

_____

_____

_____

12. What conclusion can be drawn about the early civilizations that developed in the Andes and the Pampas?

_____

_____

_____

_____

13. What conclusion can you draw about the system of mercantilism set up by Spain?

_____

_____

_____

_____

Essay

14. Summarize how the economic history of the Andes and the Pampas influences the economies of countries in the region today.

_____

_____

_____

_____

_____

_____

_____

_____

_____

_____

_____

_____

Chapter Tests

CHAPTER

7 Brazil

Test A

Key Terms

Complete each statement.

1. The _____ is the land drained by the Amazon River.

2. The outskirts of Brazilian cities are filled with slums called _____.

3. A(n) _____ economy is based on sending goods to other nations.

4. People who wanted to end slavery were called _____.

5. _____, a fuel that can be made form sugar cane, is allowing Brazil to reduce its dependence on oil.

6. Brazil has a(n) _____, in which the prices of goods are set by demand, not by the government.

Key Ideas

Identify the choice that best completes the statement or answers the question.

_____ 7. What type of land covers over half the country of Brazil?
   a. Grassland
   b. Farmland
   c. Forest
   d. Wetland

_____ 8. Why did the Portuguese first bring enslaved Africans to Brazil?
   a. To trade with them for brazilwood
   b. To work on sugar plantations
   c. To work on coffee plantations
   d. To work in gold and diamond mines

_____ 9. The first emperor of Brazil was
   a. a general who led a coup against the Portuguese.
   b. a wealthy coffee-grower.
   c. a native who seized power from the Europeans.
   d. the son of the king of Portugal.

_____ 10. What is the festival celebrated in Brazil with several days of parades, music, and dance, which combines religious traditions of southern Europe with the music and dance of Africa and the Americas?
   a. Capoeira
   b. Lent
   c. Carnival
   d. Curitiba

_____ 11. Brazil's membership in MERCOSUR means that it
   a. sends peacekeeping troops to war-torn areas of the continent.
   b. will provide economic aid to developing nations.
   c. is committed to free trade with neighboring countries.
   d. works with other oil exporters to set prices and control production.

Chapter Tests

CHAPTER

7 **Brazil** Test A

Critical Thinking

12. What type of climate supports Brazil's huge rain forest?

_____

_____

_____

_____

13. How did a boom in Brazil's coffee production help lead to changes in the country's government in the late 1800s?

_____

_____

_____

_____

14. What are some benefits and drawbacks to cutting down trees in the Amazon rain forest?

_____

_____

_____

_____

Essay

15. Why has it been so difficult to stop destruction of the Amazon rain forest, and what else might be done to stop it?

_____

_____

_____

_____

_____

_____

_____

_____

_____

_____

Chapter Tests

CHAPTER

7 Brazil

Test B

Key Terms

Complete each statement.

1. A parklike landscape of grasslands is called a(n) _____.

2. The upper level of rain forest trees, called the _____, prevents most of the sun's rays from reaching the ground.

3. An overthrow of the government is called a(n) _____.

4. Curitiba has reduced car traffic and trash while creating a parklike environment through careful _____.

5. A period of rapid economic growth followed by a sharp downturn is called a _____ and _____ cycle.

6. Programs designed to help the poor are called _____.

Key Ideas

Identify the choice that best completes the statement or answers the question.

_____ 7. The largest city in Brazil is
   a. Brasilia.
   b. Manaus.
   c. Rio de Janeiro.
   d. São Paulo.

_____ 8. What kind of economy did the Portuguese set up in Brazil?
   a. A boom economy
   b. An import economy
   c. A bust economy
   d. An export economy

_____ 9. Where does African heritage remain strongest in Brazil?
   a. In the rain forests
   b. Along the northeast coast
   c. Along the southeast coast
   d. In the Brazilian highlands

_____ 10. Today, Brazil's economy is best described as
   a. a market economy.
   b. a command economy.
   c. a mixed economy.
   d. an export economy.

_____ 11. Which of the following is the same when comparing the political system in Brazil to that of the United States?
   a. An executive branch headed by a president
   b. A minimum voting age of 21
   c. A Congress with three houses
   d. A legislature that decides court cases

Chapter Tests

CHAPTER

7 Brazil

Test B

Critical Thinking

12. How does the Amazon rain forest's location on the equator affect its climate?

_____

_____

_____

_____

13. What effect did a series of booms and busts have on Brazil's economy?

_____

_____

_____

_____

14. What steps is Brazil taking to deal with pollution?

_____

_____

_____

_____

Essay

15. Did Portuguese colonization bring bigger changes to the physical or human geography of Brazil? Explain your answer.

_____

_____

_____

_____

_____

_____

_____

_____

_____

_____

_____

_____

_____

Chapter Tests

CHAPTER 8

Ancient and Medieval Europe

Test A

Key Terms

Complete each statement.

1. Under the statesman Pericles, Athens became the world's first _____, or government in which citizens take part directly in the day-to-day affairs of government.

2. The two main groups in the Roman republic were the _____, or the wealthy aristocrats, and the plebeians, or all the remaining citizens.

3. The period of stability known as the _____, which lasted for about 200 years, began under the rule of Augustus.

4. Feudalism is the system of mutual rights and duties that connect _____ and _____ to each other.

5. The _____ were a series of military expeditions to take the Holy Land from the Muslims.

Key Ideas

Identify the choice that best completes the statement or answers the question.

_____ 6. As trade helped spread Greek culture and brought other cultures to Greece, it became a _____, or center of new ideas.
  a. colony
  b. cultural hearth
  c. oligarchy
  d. peninsula

_____ 7. During the time of the Roman republic, the tribunes played a crucial role in the government by
  a. representing the rights of the plebeians.
  b. recruiting soldiers for the army.
  c. reporting the news in the marketplace.
  d. passing laws for all citizens.

_____ 8. One difference between the Christian church in the east and the Christian church in the west was that priests in the eastern Church
  a. were not allowed to marry.
  b. reported to the patriarch of Rome.
  c. could marry.
  d. spoke Latin instead of Greek.

_____ 9. The Magna Carta was the first step toward England's
  a. large cities.
  b. war with France.
  c. merchant guilds.
  d. more democratic government.

Chapter Tests

CHAPTER

8

Ancient and
Medieval Europe

Test A

Critical Thinking

10. How did geography play a part in shaping Greek civilization, especially city-states?

_____

_____

_____

_____

11. How did Charlemagne change Europe?

_____

_____

_____

_____

12. Why were Italian trade centers important?

_____

_____

_____

_____

Essay

13. What was the classical period of Greece and what were some of the achievements in art, science, and philosophy made during this period?

_____

_____

_____

_____

_____

_____

_____

_____

_____

_____

_____

CHAPTER

8

Ancient and Medieval Europe

Test B

Key Terms

Complete each statement.

1. The fortified towns built by the Mycenaeans gradually developed into

   _____, which are cities or towns that control nearby areas.

2. Greeks studied _____ to try to understand their world through logic and reason.

3. The Ancient Roman government was a _____ democracy, where citizens elect other citizens to make political decisions for them.

4. Following the Great _____, or split, of 1054, the Byzantine church became the Eastern (or Greek) Orthodox Church.

5. The primary difference between the concepts of feudalism and manorialism is that feudalism was a legal relationship, and that manorialism was a(n)

   _____ system.

Key Ideas

Identify the choice that best completes the statement or answers the question.

_____ 6. Greece's economy prospered thanks to
   a. the arts.
   b. philosophy.
   c. trade.
   d. architecture.

_____ 7. In Athens, the system of government became a direct democracy, in which the people participated directly in government. In the Roman republic, citizens participated in government
   a. in the exact same way.
   b. through meetings held in the marketplace.
   c. by taking turns serving as consul.
   d. by choosing representatives who made decisions and laws.

_____ 8. Compasses and _____ were two new technologies that Europe gained from contact with the Muslim world.
   a. clocks
   b. astrolabes
   c. cannons
   d. eyeglasses

_____ 9. Nation-building began in Europe as a result of war and the
   a. end of Muslim rule.
   b. growth of cities.
   c. Black Death.
   d. Magna Carta.

Chapter Tests

CHAPTER

Ancient and Medieval Europe

Test B

Critical Thinking

10. What event happened in A.D. 312 that sped up the spread of Christianity in the Roman Empire?

_____

_____

_____

_____

11. In what ways did the Christian church play a key role in medieval life?

_____

_____

_____

_____

12. How did the Black Death affect Europe?

_____

_____

_____

_____

Essay

13. What do you think were the most important reasons the Romans could grow from shepherd villages in central Italy into a mighty global empire?

_____

_____

_____

_____

_____

_____

_____

_____

_____

CHAPTER

Europe in Modern Times

Test A

Key Terms

Complete each statement.

1. The artistic technique that allows artists to portray a three-dimensional space on a flat surface is called _____.

2. Explorers searched for the _____, or route between the Atlantic and the Pacific along the northern coast of North America.

3. At first, the Industrial Revolution brought pollution, long working hours, _____, and poor living conditions to society.

4. At the end of World War I, the Allies forced Germany to sign the _____, which humiliated and angered Germany.

5. During the late 1900s, a global economy developed as foreign trade and _____ grew.

Key Ideas

Identify the choice that best completes the statement or answers the question.

_____ 6. The philosophy that emphasizes individual accomplishment and serving the people of this world as opposed to focusing on religion is known as
   a. humanism.
   b. reformation.
   c. perspective.
   d. classical influence.

_____ 7. Advances in science from the Scientific Revolution were applied to human affairs during the
   a. Industrial Revolution.
   b. French Revolution.
   c. Enlightenment.
   d. Age of Exploration.

_____ 8. During the Great Depression, the United States put tariffs on imported farm products to protect the country's
   a. stock markets.
   b. investors.
   c. farmers.
   d. banks.

_____ 9. By 2008, 27 countries were members of the
   a. European Union.
   b. Marshall Plan.
   c. Iron Curtain.
   d. Soviet Union.

Chapter Tests

CHAPTER
9 Europe in Modern Times

Test A

Critical Thinking

10. How did Renaissance thinkers and the Scientific Revolution help start the Enlightenment?

_____

_____

_____

_____

_____

11. How did the Industrial Revolution change European industry and trade?

_____

_____

_____

_____

12. Why did many Germans accept Hitler and Nazi Party rule?

_____

_____

_____

_____

_____

Essay

13. Europe faces major challenges, such as strengthening the economies of Eastern Europe, the global economy, international terrorism, migration, and energy and the environment. Which of these challenges do you think will be the most difficult to meet? Why?

_____

_____

_____

_____

_____

_____

_____

_____

_____

_____

_____

Chapter Tests

CHAPTER

9

Europe in Modern Times

Test B

Key Terms

Complete each statement.

1. Johannes Gutenberg perfected _____, which made his printing press possible.

2. The three-stage pattern of Atlantic trade between Europe, Africa, and the Americas is called _____.

3. Renaissance thinkers relied on _____ to explain the world.

4. The political system that stresses national strength, military might, and the idea that the state is more important than individuals is _____.

5. Mikhail Gorbachev loosened government control in the Soviet Union and supported greater _____ in the Soviet satellite nations of Eastern Europe.

Key Ideas

Identify the choice that best completes the statement or answers the question.

_____ 6. After the Protestant Reformation, the Catholic church began to respond to the reformers' criticisms by beginning the
   a. Inquisition.
   b. Secular Reformation.
   c. 95 Theses.
   d. Catholic Reformation.

_____ 7. The combination of scientific ideas from the Scientific Revolution and political ideas from the Enlightenment led to a period of social upheaval and
   a. colonial expansion.
   b. violent change.
   c. industrial expansion.
   d. absolutist monarchs.

_____ 8. Thomas Newcomen and James Watt both invented
   a. electric light bulbs.
   b. gravity detectors.
   c. navigation instruments.
   d. steam engines.

_____ 9. A visible symbol of the Cold War division between East and West was the
   a. Soviet Union.
   b. Marshall Plan.
   c. United Nations.
   d. Berlin Wall.

Chapter Tests

CHAPTER

9

Europe in Modern Times

Test B

Critical Thinking

10. What was the Columbian Exchange?

_____

_____

_____

_____

11. Why were antidemocratic leaders able to take power in the Soviet Union and Italy after World War I?

_____

_____

_____

_____

12. How was Europe divided after World War II and during the Cold War?

_____

_____

_____

_____

Essay

13. What is the relationship between the Age of Empire and World War 1?

_____

_____

_____

_____

_____

_____

_____

_____

_____

_____

_____

Chapter Tests

CHAPTER

10 Western Europe

Test A

Key Terms

Complete each statement.

1. A thick forest of coniferous trees, called a _____, is found in areas such as Scandinavia.

2. Acid rain is one effect of _____.

3. Britain's use of the _____ as its currency instead of the euro shows that Britain prefers limited ties to the European Union.

4. The _____ ensures that French products, such as wine, cheese, and grains, reach people around the world.

5. The Southern European nations of Spain, Andorra, and Portugal are located on the _____.

6. Portugal's economic growth since it joined the EU is largely the result of Portugal's efforts to _____ its economy.

Key Ideas

Identify the choice that best completes the statement or answers the question.

_____ 7. What made the Rhine River one of Europe's most polluted rivers?
   a. Urbanization
   b. Loess
   c. Industrial waste
   d. Natural gas

_____ 8. Some Norwegians feel that the EU's structure is not democratic. As a result, these people probably favor _____ ties with the European Union.
   a. cultural
   b. democratic
   c. stronger
   d. limited

_____ 9. Which of the following is the correct term for converting government-owned industries to private ownership?
   a. Reunification
   b. Privatization
   c. Gross national product
   d. Neutrality

_____ 10. Which of the following industries is an example of the part of the economy known as the service sector?
   a. Telecommunications
   b. Textile production
   c. Computer chip manufacturing
   d. Porcelain production

CHAPTER
10 Western Europe   Test A

Critical Thinking

11. Why are Western Europe's most heavily populated areas within 100 miles of the coast?

_____

_____

_____

12. How does warm water brought to Europe's western coast by the Atlantic Ocean affect the region's climate?

_____

_____

_____

_____

13. Why are many Germans both proud and uneasy about their culture?

_____

_____

_____

Essay

14. What problems does immigration cause in Europe, and how might European countries deal with these problems?

_____

_____

_____

_____

_____

_____

_____

_____

_____

_____

Chapter Tests

CHAPTER

10 Western Europe   Test B

Key Terms

Complete each statement.

1. In order to preserve land for forests, recreation, and growing food, most countries limit the growth of _____.

2. _____ is the total value of all goods and services produced and sold in a country in a year.

3. When the Berlin Wall fell in 1989, East Germany and West Germany began the process of _____.

4. Switzerland has a long history of _____, which has led to Switzerland's difficult relationships with international organizations.

5. Granada, Spain, which blends Christian, Jewish, and Muslim traditions, is an example of _____, or the spread of culture.

6. The process of sending an immigrant back to his or her home country is called _____.

Key Ideas

Identify the choice that best completes the statement or answers the question.

_____ 7. Which feature of Western Europe helps make public transportation networks possible?
   a. Temperate climate
   b. Pollution
   c. Rich farmland
   d. Large urban areas

_____ 8. What is the system of government in England called?
   a. House of Commons and House of Lords
   b. Constitutional monarchy
   c. Democracy
   d. British Constitution

_____ 9. What industry is one of West Central Europe's largest and most important industries?
   a. Skiing
   b. Tourism
   c. Electrical machinery
   d. Book publishing

_____ 10. The nations of Southern Europe have enjoyed strong growth as members of
   a. the European Union.
   b. NATO.
   c. Mediterranean culture.
   d. different religious groups.

CHAPTER

10 Western Europe   Test B

Critical Thinking

11. Compare and contrast Western Europe's Arctic climate to its Mediterranean climate.

_____

_____

_____

_____

12. How does Germany's past affect the attitudes of today's Germans toward immigration and immigrants?

_____

_____

_____

_____

13. Discuss some of the reasons for economic changes experienced by Southern European countries.

_____

_____

_____

_____

Essay

14. In general, has membership in the European Union helped or hurt the countries of Western Europe?

_____

_____

_____

_____

_____

_____

_____

_____

_____

_____

_____

Chapter Tests

CHAPTER

11 Eastern Europe   Test A

Key Terms

Complete each statement.

1. The physical features of this region were shaped by a long period of lower temperatures, when much of the land was covered in snow and ice. This period is known as a(n) _____.

2. Estonia's economy has been successful because its industries have _____, or money to invest.

3. Many republics in Yugoslavia were unhappy with the Serbian government, so they began to _____, or break away, from Yugoslavia.

Key Ideas

Identify the choice that best completes the statement or answers the question.

_____ 4. As they moved, glaciers scraped up rocks and soil and then dropped these materials when they melted, creating _____ across the region.
   a. the North European Plain
   b. ridges of hills
   c. many large rivers
   d. the Carpathian Mountains

_____ 5. Mechanized farming techniques are well-suited to geographic areas that
   a. have a shortage of inexpensive labor.
   b. are closer to major urban areas.
   c. have large expanses of flat land.
   d. experience frequent flooding.

_____ 6. One reason why many people in Eastern Europe do not belong to any religion is that
   a. missionaries have been unable to reach the area.
   b. they are more concerned with Communist Party matters.
   c. religion was discouraged by the Soviet Union's government.
   d. economic hardship has made the people bitter.

_____ 7. The Polish economy began to grow in the 1990s because the government
   a. built more state-owned factories.
   b. controlled prices better.
   c. stopped new private businesses.
   d. encouraged entrepreneurs.

_____ 8. One of the worst ethnic conflicts, involving the policy of ethnic cleansing, was the war between Serbia and the province of
   a. Macedonia.   c. Montenegro.
   b. Kosovo.   d. Slovenia.

Chapter Tests

CHAPTER

11 Eastern Europe

Test A

Critical Thinking

9. How has the fall of the Soviet Union changed attitudes toward religion in some Eastern European countries?

_____

_____

_____

_____

10. How is farming in the northern part of Eastern Europe different from farming in the southern part of the region?

_____

_____

_____

_____

11. Why is membership in the European Union so important to most of the Eastern European countries today?

_____

_____

_____

_____

Essay

12. What is the energy challenge facing Eastern Europe? If one of the Eastern European presidents asked you for advice, what would you recommend as a solution?

_____

_____

_____

_____

_____

_____

_____

_____

_____

_____

_____

11 Eastern Europe   Test B

Key Terms

Complete each statement.

1. Since the 1940s there has been a revival of Jewish communities in some areas, while, in other areas, Jewish people continue to _____, or leave one area to move to another.

2. Burning coal and other fossil fuels sends chemicals into the air, and this plays a part in the production of _____.

3. Hungarians, who are different in some ways from their Eastern European neighbors, have a unique _____, or style of food.

Key Ideas

Identify the choice that best completes the statement or answers the question.

_____ 4. The 1986 explosion at the Chernobyl nuclear power plant in _____ caused a serious environmental problem.
   a. Poland   c. Ukraine
   b. Moldova   d. Belarus

_____ 5. Most of Eastern Europe has very cold winters and mild summers, which is typical of the _____ climate.
   a. Mediterranean
   b. humid subtropical
   c. continental cool summer
   d. continental warm summer

_____ 6. A nation whose industries have enough capital will be able to expand its economy because
   a. the business of the nation's government will take place in a single city.
   b. it can invest in equipment to make more goods for trade.
   c. service-sector industries will decrease in importance.
   d. the industries can overrule tariffs.

_____ 7. The first republic to secede from the country of Yugoslavia in 1990 was
   a. Slovenia.
   b. Macedonia.
   c. Croatia.
   d. Slovakia.

_____ 8. A consequence of the break-up of the country of Yugoslavia into different republics was
   a. the rise of a strong authoritarian regime aimed at re-uniting them.
   b. the founding of NATO to combat the new threat.
   c. ethnic cleansing and other efforts to create areas of only one ethnic group.
   d. enhanced trade between the new countries.

CHAPTER

11 Eastern Europe

Test B

Critical Thinking

9. In Eastern Europe, how does geography influence industry?

_____

_____

_____

_____

10. Why have Poland and the Baltic nations been among the most economically successful countries in Eastern Europe?

_____

_____

_____

_____

11. What has been the impact of ethnic conflict on the Balkan nations?

_____

_____

_____

_____

Essay

12. If you were an entrepreneur, which of the Eastern European countries might be the best place to start your new business? Explain your reasoning.

_____

_____

_____

_____

_____

_____

_____

_____

_____

_____

_____

CHAPTER

12 Russia

Test A

Key Terms

Complete each statement.

1. Famous for its 29 active volcanoes, the _____ lies at the eastern edge of the Russian Far East.

2. South of Moscow, the countryside consists mainly of vast areas of grassland, also known as _____.

3. Vladimir Lenin led to power a branch of the Social Democrats called the _____ and introduced communism.

4. Many believe the source of Putin's authoritative style is his involvement with the Soviet era secret police, known as the _____.

5. Russia is using its status as a(n) _____, or an extermely powerful nation, and its wealth of natural resources to be an important player on the world stage.

Key Ideas

Identify the choice that best completes the statement or answers the question.

_____ 6. As a result of its vast reserves of _____, Russia has become a wealthy nation in recent years.
   a. timber
   b. coal
   c. oil and gas
   d. cobalt

_____ 7. East Slavs who migrated to the Dnieper region encountered invaders from Asia, including Huns, Avars, Magyars, and
   a. Vikings.
   b. Finns.
   c. Goths.
   d. Khazars.

_____ 8. Real reform in the Soviet Union began under _____, who introduced the policies of glasnost and perestroika.
   a. Vladimir Lenin
   b. Josef Stalin
   c. Mikhail Gorbachev
   d. Vladimir Putin

_____ 9. During his terms in office, Vladimir Putin has made changes that have resulted in Russia becoming the world leader in
   a. personal income growth.
   b. reducing crime.
   c. the production of oil and gas.
   d. reducing poverty.

Chapter Tests

CHAPTER
12 Russia

Critical Thinking

10. How are climate and population density in Russia related?

_____

_____

_____

_____

11. How did the Communists come to power in Russia?

_____

_____

_____

_____

12. Compare and contrast the way communism works with the way democratic capitalism works. Include the roles of the government, political leadership, and who makes political decisions.

_____

_____

_____

_____

Essay

13. How did the practice of communism in Russia differ from the theory of how communism is supposed to work?

_____

_____

_____

_____

_____

_____

_____

_____

_____

_____

_____

Chapter Tests

CHAPTER

12 Russia

Test B

Key Terms

Complete each statement.

1. The largest part of Russia, which is called _____, stretches eastward from the Ural Mountains to the Pacific Ocean.

2. Prince Ivan III began calling himself _____, a term derived from the Latin *Caesar* or king.

3. During the Russian revolution, Lenin and the Bolsheviks used Marx's ideas to gain the support of workers' councils known as _____, so Lenin could claim the Bolsheviks represented the voices of the working class.

4. Josef Stalin wanted agriculture to be controlled by groups instead of by individuals, a policy known as _____.

5. One of the powers of government that the Russian government exercises is to _____, or suppress, news stories that it does not like.

Key Ideas

Identify the choice that best completes the statement or answers the question.

_____ 6. European Russia is separated from Asiatic Russia by the
   a. West Siberian Plain.
   b. Caucasus Mountains.
   c. Ural Mountains.
   d. Caspian Sea.

_____ 7. Most of Russia's densely settled areas lie _____ of the Ural Mountains; most of the rest of Russia is sparsely populated.
   a. east
   b. west
   c. north
   d. south

_____ 8. Although there had been _____ during the Soviet era, it has become an epidemic in the years that followed.
   a. corruption
   b. centralization
   c. economic growth
   d. authoritarianism

_____ 9. People all over the world, whether they know it or not, depend on Russian
   a. nuclear reactors.
   b. attitudes toward climate change.
   c. membership in NATO.
   d. oil and gas.

CHAPTER

12 Russia

Test B

Critical Thinking

10. Describe some of Russia's resources and name two challenges to resource development.

_____

_____

_____

_____

11. How did Russia change under the rule of Catherine II?

_____

_____

_____

_____

_____

12. How did Vladimir Putin bring significant improvement to the daily life of Russians during his two terms as president?

_____

_____

_____

_____

Essay

13. Given Russia's geography and history, what opportunities or problems do you predict Russia will face in the rest of this century as it attempts to increase its political and economic power?

_____

_____

_____

_____

_____

_____

_____

_____

_____

_____

_____

Chapter Tests

Final Test
Western Hemisphere

Multiple Choice
Identify the choice that best completes the statement or answers the question.

_____ 1. What causes the seasons?
    a. Earth moving closer to or further away from the sun as it makes it yearly journey around the sun
    b. Changes in the intensity of the sun's energy output
    c. Earth's tilt causing different amounts of light to fall on certain areas at different times
    d. Changes in the core temperature of Earth

_____ 2. Time in the region surrounding the Prime Meridian is sometimes called
    a. Prime Time.
    b. London Mean Time.
    c. Global Standard Time.
    d. Universal Time.

_____ 3. The _____ on a map allows you to measure the real-world distance between two points on the map's surface.
    a. compass rose
    b. contour lines
    c. scale
    d. topography

_____ 4. Which of the following is likely to be found only on a special purpose map?
    a. Boundaries between nations
    b. Oceans
    c. Continents
    d. Streets

_____ 5. Geographers use the term *place* to describe which of the following?
    a. The mix of human and nonhuman features at a given location
    b. The altitude of a given position
    c. A specific latitude and longitude
    d. A street address with a zip code

_____ 6. The theme of human-environment interaction includes
    a. only ways in which humans harm the environment through pollution.
    b. only natural disasters such as earthquakes and hurricanes.
    c. both how the environment affects humans and how humans affect the environment.
    d. only events that have happened since the Industrial Revolution.

_____ 7. It takes 365 1/4 days for the Earth to complete one full _____ around the sun.
    a. rotation
    b. revolution
    c. lunar month
    d. ecliptic

Final Test

Final Test
Western Hemisphere

_____ 8. Earth completes one _____, or full turn, every 24 hours.
   a. rotation
   b. revolution
   c. lunar month
   d. ecliptic

_____ 9. Which of the following describes the Earth's mantle?
   a. A rocky crust containing both mountains and seafloor
   b. Solid and metallic
   c. A mixture of solid and liquid matter
   d. Solid, but so hot that it can flow like a liquid

_____ 10. Which of the following is one process involved as rivers carve valleys between mountains or hills?
   a. deposition   **c.** weathering
   b. erosion   **d.** superposition

_____ 11. The high latitudes, also known as the _____, get less direct sunlight because the sun is near or below the horizon all year-round.
   a. tropics
   b. temperate zones
   c. low latitudes
   d. polar zones

_____ 12. _____ affects climate by affecting the air temperature near it.
   a. Wind   **c.** Water
   b. Precipitation   **d.** Current

_____ 13.

According to the graphs, precipitation in Bangalore, India
   a. falls mostly from November to April.
   b. falls about the same year-round.
   c. falls as snow in January to March.
   d. falls mostly from May to October.

Final Test
Western Hemisphere

_____ 14. An ecosystem is a network of _____ that depend on one another and their environment for survival.
   a. plants
   b. living things
   c. animals
   d. people

_____ 15. Which of the following are considered sources of clean energy?
   a. Coal
   b. Wind
   c. Wood
   d. Ethanol

_____ 16. One thing people can do to help protect the environment is to
   a. use fertilizer to help grow food.
   b. try to use less oil.
   c. encourage economic growth.
   d. drill for oil only deep in the ocean.

_____ 17. The difference between wants and reality creates _____, or having a limited quantity of resources to meet unlimited wants.
   a. supply
   b. scarcity
   c. economy
   d. choices

_____ 18. The money earned by selling goods and services is called
   a. profit.
   b. revenue.
   c. living expense.
   d. salary.

_____ 19. The _____ is the total value of all goods and services produced in a country in a year.
   a. gross domestic product (GDP)
   b. average national income
   c. export-import ratio
   d. federal budget deficit

_____ 20. A tariff causes a barrier to free trade because
   a. it is charged at the point of export.
   b. it only applies to services.
   c. it makes the price of a good higher to a consumer.
   d. it can be applied to countries regardless of whether or not they have joined free-trade zones.

Final Test
Western Hemisphere

_____ **21.** A bond is a certificate issued by a company or government promising to
     a. pay back borrowed money with interest.
     b. loan money to the bondholder.
     c. give partial ownership of a company's assets.
     d. share in any profits or losses that occur.

_____ **22.** Demographers are scientists who study
     a. weather and climate.
     b. pollution.
     c. human populations.
     d. ocean currents.

_____ **23.** Using up resources is one of the negative effects of
     a. the birthrate.
     b. the death rate.
     c. the infant mortality rate.
     d. rapid population growth.

_____ **24.** The distribution of the world's population on Earth's surface is best described as
     a. even.
     b. thick.
     c. uneven.
     d. thin.

_____ **25.** Scientists believe that more than 50,000 years ago, some early humans migrated from _____ to Asia and then to other continents.
     a. Europe
     b. Africa
     c. North America
     d. Antarctica

_____ **26.** In recent years, millions of Chinese workers have moved from _____ areas to _____ areas.
     a. urban; rural
     b. coastal; mountain
     c. rural; urban
     d. northern; southern

_____ **27.** The beliefs, customs, practices, and behavior of a particular nation or group is that nation's or group's
     a. norm.
     b. culture region.
     c. cultural landscape.
     d. culture.

Final Test

Final Test
Western Hemisphere

____ 28. The most basic unit of any society is the
    a. family.
    b. society.
    c. social structure.
    d. extended family.

____ 29. A set of spoken sounds, written symbols, or hand gestures used by people to communicate is a
    a. culture.
    b. society.
    c. language.
    d. cultural trait.

____ 30. The world's major religions each began in lands that are part of the continent of
    a. North America.
    b. Africa.
    c. Asia.
    d. Europe.

____ 31. Several things that all religions have in common are prayers, rituals, and
    a. Christmas.
    b. religious holidays.
    c. special foods.
    d. one god.

____ 32. _____ spread cultural traits because they bring cultural traditions with them to their new homeland.
    a. Traders
    b. Explorers
    c. Migrants
    d. Native Americans

____ 33. A group of people who have the power to make and enforce laws for a country or area is always called a
    a. government.
    b. limited government.
    c. unlimited government.
    d. tyranny.

____ 34. Today the majority of states are
    a. city-states.
    b. nation-states.
    c. empires.
    d. monarchies.

Final Test

Final Test
Western Hemisphere

_____ **35.** Which of the following lists the levels of the federal system of government in the correct order, starting with the top level of government and ending with the bottom level?
a. Central, regional, local
b. Regional, local, central
c. Central, local, regional
d. Regional, central, local

_____ **36.** Which of the following is a power that belongs to the executive branch of the U.S. government?
a. Deciding whether a law is constitutional or not
b. Levying taxes on the citizens of the United States
c. Conducting the foreign affairs of the United States
d. Passing laws for the good of the American people

_____ **37.** Which of the following organizations fights disease by providing food and relief services to victims of war and natural disaster?
a. Amnesty International
b. World Health Organization
c. United Nations
d. International Red Cross and Red Crescent Movement

_____ **38.** All political power in the United States comes from
a. citizens.
b. interest groups.
c. political parties.
d. government.

_____ **39.**

Column A	Column B
Book	Letter
Movie	Diary
Encyclopedia article	Photograph

In the chart above, what are the items in Column A?
a. Primary sources
b. Secondary sources
c. Artifacts
d. Biases

_____ **40.** A period is a length of time singled out because
a. it is a measure based on units of 1000 years.
b. not much happened between two important events.
c. it aligns with the average life-span of a human at that time.
d. a specific event or development that happened during that time.

Final Test
Western Hemisphere

_____ **41.** Which of the following is an example of an artifact?
  a. A toy carved from sticks
  b. A folk-song by an anonymous composer, which old musicians teach to younger musicians
  c. A legend about a hero founding a new city that is passed down by word of mouth
  d. An old custom people follow without knowing the original reason for it

_____ **42.** _____ is a community's cultural and historical background, passed down in spoken stories and songs.
  a. Archaeology
  b. Oral tradition
  c. Geography
  d. Economics.

_____ **43.** A historical map is an example of a
  a. political map.
  b. Mercator projection map.
  c. special-purpose map.
  d. political map,

_____ **44.** Prior to the American Revolution, most large plantations were located
  a. near the cities.
  b. in the South.
  c. in the North.
  d. along the coast.

_____ **45.** Which of the four major regions of the United States was settled last by U.S. citizens?
  a. Northeast
  b. South
  c. Midwest
  d. West

_____ **46.** The heartland of Canada, where the majority of Canadians live and work, is located
  a. around the Great Lakes and St. Lawrence River.
  b. around Hudson Bay.
  c. along Canada's Atlantic Coast.
  d. near the Arctic Circle.

_____ **47.** With which Act did Britain allow religious freedom and French laws?
  a. The Quebec Act
  b. Act of Union
  c. Religious Freedom Act
  d. British North America Act

Final Test
Western Hemisphere

_____ **48.** Agriculture in the Americas began when native peoples began to grow
  a. tobacco.
  b. maize.
  c. cotton.
  d. apple trees.

_____ **49.** What is one reason that only about one-fifth of Mexico's land is available to be used for farming?
  a. Because the soil is too damp
  b. Because of a lack of natural resources
  c. Because of mountains, poor soils, and dry climates
  d. Because there are too many rivers in Mexico

_____ **50.** An isthmus is
  a. a narrow waterway between two land masses.
  b. a point of land surrounded by water on three sides.
  c. an inlet protected from ocean storms.
  d. a strip of land with water on both sides that connects two larger bodies of land.

_____ **51.** In Central America, a hacienda was
  a. a wealthy landowner who controlled the local economy and the votes of peasants living nearby.
  b. the leader of a military rebellion.
  c. a new plan for a government.
  d. a huge farm or ranch.

Economies of Caribbean South America	
Country	**GDP per Capita**
Colombia	$8,900
Venezuela	$13,500
Guyana	$3,900
Suriname	$8,900

_____ **53.** SOURCE: *CIA World Factbook*
  Which country in Caribbean South America has the most productive economy?
  a. Colombia
  b. Venezuela
  c. Guyana
  d. Suriname

Final Test
Western Hemisphere

_____ **52.** In 1976, what did the government of Venezuela do to the oil industry?
  a. It installed *caudillos* as leaders.
  b. It sent in paramilitaries.
  c. It introduced austerity measures.
  d. It nationalized the industry.

_____ **54.** What language is spoken by most people in the Andes and Pampas regions?
  a. English
  b. Spanish
  c. Indigenous languages
  d. Italian

_____ **55.** Voters in Chile amended the constitution in 1989 because they
  a. wanted to bring democracy back to the country.
  b. felt a stronger central government was needed.
  c. were struggling with a large national debt that was owed to many different foreign countries.
  d. needed to clarify the division between church and state.

_____ **56.** The Portuguese traded with Native Americans in the Amazon for brazilwood because it
  a. was a sturdy building material.
  b. could be used in guitars and other musical instruments.
  c. repelled water.
  d. produced a red dye.

_____ **57.** In the late 1800s, which group arose to become the most politically powerful group in Brazil?
  a. Sugarcane farmers
  b. Gold miners
  c. Diamond miners
  d. Coffee farmers

_____ **58.** Because they had so little _____, the ancient Greeks depended on the sea for much of their food.
  a. farmland
  b. rainfall
  c. mountainous area
  d. coastline

_____ **59.** Rome turned conquered people into allies using military strength and
  a. diplomacy.
  b. plebeians.
  c. patricians.
  d. tributes.

Final Test

Final Test
Western Hemisphere

_____ **60.** One element of Roman law that still appears in our system of government today is the system of _____, which ensures that no one branch of government becomes too powerful.
a. checks and balances
b. Twelve Tables of laws
c. patricians and plebeians
d. consuls and tribal assemblies

_____ **61.** The teachings of Jesus of Nazareth became the basis of a religion called _____, which gradually spread across the entire Roman Empire within 300 years.
a. Christianity
b. Judaism
c. *Pax Romana*
d. representative democracy

_____ **62.** In exchange for loyalty, kings granted land to lords, who, in turn, granted smaller parcels of that land to knights under the system called
a. manorialism.
b. the rule of law.
c. Charlemagne.
d. feudalism.

_____ **63.** Pope Leo III, a Christian pope, crowned Charlemagne, a _____ ruler, as Holy Roman Emperor.
a. Byzantine
b. Frankish
c. Viking
d. Russian

_____ **64.** As feudalism ended and trade increased, the movement of people and ideas throughout Europe led to a period of renewed interest in art and learning, called the
a. Catholic Reformation.
b. Inquisition.
c. Renaissance.
d. Reformation.

_____ **65.** A book describing the wealth and wonders of Asia, written by the Italian merchant _____, increased many Europeans' interest in the riches of Asia.
a. Henry the Navigator
b. Marco Polo
c. Christopher Columbus
d. Vasco da Gama

Final Test
Western Hemisphere

_____ **66.** Some Spanish explorers in the New World took the land they seized and use it to set up large commercial farms, called _____, on Caribbean islands.
   a. conquistadors
   b. trade routes
   c. plantations
   d. colonies

_____ **67.** The four causes of World War I were alliances, nationalism, imperialism, and
   a. communism.
   b. militarism.
   c. fascism.
   d. the Great Depression.

_____ **68.** During World War II, the members of the Axis Powers were Germany, Italy, and
   a. Japan.
   b. the United States.
   c. France.
   d. Britain.

_____ **69.** After the Cold War, East German factories were outdated and inefficient and many of them were
   a. Soviet satellites.
   b. rebuilt.
   c. closed.
   d. American-owned.

_____ **70.** The physical feature of Western Europe where most major cities are found is
   a. the plains.
   b. the glacier.
   c. the tundra.
   d. the taiga.

_____ **71.** The idea of democracy began in which nation?
   a. Spain
   b. Portugal
   c. Italy
   d. Greece

_____ **72.** Which of the following describes a system of basic services for citizens at every stage of life?
   a. Cradle-to-grave system
   b. Social services benefits
   c. Gross domestic product
   d. Pensions and healthcare

Final Test

Final Test
Western Hemisphere

_____ 73. What is the European Union?
   a. An international organization that exists to make sure that world war would never happen again
   b. An international organization, also known as the ECC, made up of 6 European countries
   c. An international organization of many countries that works to expand prosperity
   d. An international organization that supports sports teams in many European countries

_____ 74. Many immigrants hide from officials in their new country because they fear
   a. immigration.
   b. cultural diffusion.
   c. diversification.
   d. deportation.

_____ 75. Which of the following has contributed to Estonia's success in moving beyond the former Soviet Union?
   a. The creation of a large army
   b. The development of an autocratic system of government, with the president holding all power.
   c. Abandoning the Communist command economic system in favor of a market economic system
   d. Strict quotas for producing goods

_____ 76. One factor contributing to the slow economic growth of Ukraine when compared to other countries in the region is
   a. corruption.
   b. available natural resources.
   c. bad weather.
   d. military conflict.

_____ 77. In many areas of northern Russia, a layer of _____ lies beneath the tundra or the taiga.
   a. coal
   b. peat moss
   c. permafrost
   d. ground water

_____ 78. Communism is a political and social system based on a theory under which all forms of industry would be owned by
   a. capitalists.
   b. the people as a whole.
   c. the tsar.
   d. individuals.

Final Test
Western Hemisphere

Short Answer

79. How has the U.S. economy changed over the past fifty years?

_____

_____

_____

_____

_____

80. Compare and contrast Canada's national government with that of the United States.

_____

_____

_____

_____

_____

81. Compare and contrast Mexico's economy in the early 1900s with its economy now.

_____

_____

_____

_____

_____

82. Why were the economies of the newly independent nations of Caribbean South America weak?

_____

_____

_____

_____

_____

83. How did Portuguese colonization change the physical geography of Brazil?

_____

_____

_____

_____

Final Test

Final Test
Western Hemisphere

84. How was Roman society divided?

_____

_____

_____

_____

_____

85. What were two Enlightenment ideas that influenced Americans' view of government?

_____

_____

_____

_____

_____

86. How might the viewpoints of larger countries in the European Union differ from the viewpoints of smaller countries?

_____

_____

_____

_____

_____

87. In Eastern Europe, how does geography influence industry?

_____

_____

_____

_____

_____

88. What challenges does Russia face as it finds its place in today's world?

_____

_____

_____

_____

_____

Final Test

Name _____ Class _____ Date _____

Final Test
Western Hemisphere

Essay

89. Explain how wind and water relate to maritime climates.

_____
_____
_____
_____
_____
_____
_____
_____
_____
_____
_____
_____

90. What role do families play in the culture of a society, and how might families either preserve or change culture?

_____
_____
_____
_____
_____
_____
_____
_____
_____
_____
_____
_____
_____
_____
_____

Final Test

Copyright © Pearson Education, Inc., or its affiliates. All Rights Reserved.
111

Final Test
Western Hemisphere

91. Apply your knowledge of the five themes of geography to create a description of your
hometown that includes examples of each theme. (You may give your hometown's
relative location rather than its absolute location.) How does using each theme
improve your description?

_____

_____

_____

_____

_____

_____

_____

_____

_____

_____

_____

_____

_____

_____

_____

92. Would a pure market economy be better than a mixed economy? Explain the reasons
for your answer.

_____

_____

_____

_____

_____

_____

_____

_____

_____

_____

_____

_____

_____

_____

Final Test

Core Concepts Part 1 Tools of Geography Test A

Key Terms 1. degrees 2. hemisphere 3. aerial photographs, satellite photographs (both acceptable) 4. geographic information systems 5. projections 6. locator map 7. compass rose 8. political map 9. relative location 10. region

Key Ideas 11. C 12. A 13. D

Critical Thinking 14. A map has a flexible scale, can focus in on a single area in greater detail than a globe, and provides clearer labels for roads and other features than an aerial photograph. 15. Measure the distance between the two points on the map, then use the map's scale bar to convert the measured distance into actual distance. 16. Answers will vary. Students should note significant features such as general climate, high or low population, flat or hilly terrain, and so forth. Students should address the geographic theme of place with their descriptions.

Essay 17. Answers will vary.

Core Concepts Part 1 Tools of Geography Test B

Key Terms 1. latitude 2. longitude 3. distortion 4. satellite images 5. key 6. scale bar 7. physical map 8. elevation 9. absolute location 10. movement

Key Ideas 11. B 12. C 13. D

Critical Thinking 14. A globe shows the entire world clearly and in fairly accurate proportions. Maps flatten and distort images. Satellite images show an exact look, which can make it hard to find information. 15. The compass rose provides basic information about cardinal directions that applies to many different types of maps, regardless of the specific information that the maps display. 16. Students should accurately describe the location of their school in relation to another building, using directions and/or distance. **Essay** 17. Answers will vary.

Core Concepts Part 2 Our Planet Earth Test A

Key Terms 1. orbit 2. equinox 3. time zones 4. crust 5. erosion 6. plateau 7. plates

Key Ideas 8. A 9. C 10. A 11. D

Critical Thinking 12. Earth's tilt remains the same as it orbits around the sun. This means that at some points during Earth's revolution, the northern hemisphere is tilted more or less directly towards the sun, receiving different amounts of sunlight at different times. These changes in the amount of sunlight cause the temperature to rise or fall, producing the seasons 13. The crust floats on top of the mantle, which is capable of movement. The heat and motion of the mantle act to push up certain portions of Earth's crust. 14. Plains, deltas, and sandy beaches are formed by the deposition of eroded material.

Essay 15. Answers will vary.

Core Concepts Part 2 Our Planet Earth Test B

Key Terms 1. axis 2. solstice 3. core 4. landforms 5. weathering 6. deposition 7. plate tectonics

Key Ideas 8. D 9. B 10. A 11. D
Critical Thinking 12. During each of these periods, one of the hemispheres is tilted closer to the Sun than the other, so they receive different amounts of sunlight and experience opposite seasons from each other 13. There would be no oxygen to breathe, and there would be no layer of gases to trap the sun's energy and keep Earth warm enough to sustain life. 14.

Mountains, hills, valleys, and plateaus are all shaped by the process of erosion.

Essay 15. Answers will vary.

Core Concepts Part 3 Climates and Ecosystems Test A

Key Terms 1. temperate zones 2. weather 3. evaporation 4. hurricane 5. savanna 6. onshore

Key Ideas 7. B 8. A 9. D 10. D

Critical Thinking 11. In the spring and summer, the Earth tilts toward the sun on its axis. As a result, the high latitudes receive more direct sunlight each day than in the fall and winter. In the winter, Earth's axis tilts the high latitudes away from the sun's energy and they get less direct sunlight each day. The temperatures go down. Winters can be bitterly cold. 12. In the tropics, the sun's heat warms the air. As this warm air rises, it loses its moisture in the form of precipitation. This cooler, drier air is pushed away by the rising warm air. When the cool, dry air is no longer rising, it begins to fall back toward the Earth. When the cool, dry air reaches Earth's surface, it produces winds that blow along the surface and pick up moisture. 13. Arid climates occur where there are steadily sinking air or winds. In arid climates, the hot, humid air rises, loses its moisture, and is pushed away. The warm, dry air sinks back to Earth's surface. These are the areas where you find hot desert regions.

Essay 14. Answers will vary.

Core Concepts Part 3 Climates and Ecosystems Test B

Key Terms 1. climate 2. evaporate 3. intertropical convergence zone (ITCZ) 4. tornadoes 5. lose their leaves 6. semiarid and arid climates

Key Ideas 7. B 8. B 9. A 10. B

Critical Thinking 11. The polar zone or high latitudes, the temperate zones or the middle latitudes, and the tropics or low latitudes are the three zones of latitude. Some zones, such as the tropics and temperate zones, are warmer than others, such as the polar zones, because different areas of the planet receive different amounts of direct sunlight. The different areas of the planet receive different amounts of direct sunlight because of the tilt of the Earth's axis. 12. As warm air rises, it cools and it loses its moisture as precipitation. The cool air is pushed away, and sinks at the edge of the tropics. It is warmed and rises again in the temperate zones. After cooling and losing its moisture once more, the air falls again at the poles. As a result, precipitation is lightest at the edge of the tropics and then near the poles. 13. Answers will vary. Possible answer: I think wind is the most important shaper of arid climates because these regions are found where dry air is sinking back to Earth's surface after losing all of most of its moisture.

Essay 14. Answers will vary.

Core Concepts Part 4 Human-Environment Interaction Test A

Key Terms 1. nonrenewable 2. natural environment 3. grassland or barren land 4. deforestation

Key Ideas 5. C 6. A 7. B 8. B 9. D

Critical Thinking 10. Colonization may impact land use by bringing new crops, new ways of farming, or new animals to a new home. For example, when Europeans colonized parts of Africa, the Americas, and Australia, they often cut down large areas of forest to clear the land for growing crops or feeding their livestock. 11. Agricultural activities would most likely take place on land used for cropland and grassland. In the United States, there is a large region in the central part of the country that is cropland or grassland. **12.** Extracting resources means taking resources out of the ecosystem or the environment. If people take too much of a resource out of an ecosystem, they can harm the ecosystem. For instance, if people cut down too many trees in a forest, they may cause deforestation. If deforestation happens, animals that live in the forest may suffer.

Essay **13.** Answers will vary.

Core Concepts Part 4 Human-Environment Interaction Test B

Key Terms **1.** environment **2.** renewable **3.** suburbs **4.** spillover

Key Ideas **5.** B **6.** A **7.** D **8.** C **9.** D

Critical Thinking **10.** In some places, large cities grew up around centers for industry. As cities grew, people used land that had been forests, cropland, or pasture, for factories and houses. **11.** Natural resources and culture are the two factors that determine how people use land. Land use can be changed by a change in natural resources. Colonization, which is the movement of new settlers into an area, may change the way land is being used. They may cut down trees to clear land for crops and livestock. Industrialization and the growth of suburbs can also change the way land is used. **12.** When people use resources to grow food or make other goods and services, they can produce pollution or damage the environment.

Essay **13.** Answers will vary.

Core Concepts Part 5 Economics and Geography Test A

Key Terms **1.** incentive **2.** Demand **3.** Profit **4.** inflation **5.** command economy **6.** developed country **7.**

productivity **8.** Exports **9.** trade barrier **10.** interest **11.** stock

Key Ideas **12.** C **13.** B **14.** D

Critical Thinking **15.** Consumers buy fewer goods and services, so production slows. **16.** The government provides services and money to businesses and households. It receives resources, goods and services, and money in the form of taxes from businesses and households. **17.** Improved technology can create new products and make it easier for people to do business, which helps increase development.

Essay **18.** Answers will vary.

Core Concepts Part 5 Economic and Geography Test B

Key Terms **1.** supply **2.** market **3.** specialization **4.** competition **5.** market economy **6.** Development **7.** Technology **8.** Imports **9.** free trade **10.** Credit **11.** Investing

Key Ideas **12.** D **13.** C **14.** A

Critical Thinking **15.** Recession can lead to unemployment because when the economy's growth declines, demand decreases as well. As demand decreases, fewer people are needed to produce goods and services, leading to unemployment. **16.** Both Japan and Cuba have mixed economies. However, Japan's economy is close to a pure market economy and Cuba's economy is close to a pure command economy. **17.** Improving education and training increases workers' skill and knowledge, which gets them higher wages. More people with higher wages leads to increased development.

Essay **18.** Answers will vary.

Core Concepts Part 6 Population and Movement Test A

Key Terms 1. birth rate 2. population density 3. internal 4. pull factors 5. slums 6. urbanization 7. suburban

Key Ideas 8. B 9. B 10. B 11. A

Critical Thinking 12. Population can grow faster than the supply of food, water, medicine, and other resources. When this happens, starvation and disease can cause a high infant mortality rate. 13. Immigrants come to the United States for jobs, freedom, the chance for a better life, and other reasons 14. Urbanization is the movement of people from rural areas to urban areas. People who are already residents of the city have their lives disrupted by traffic, pollution, and increasing housing costs.

Essay 15. Answers will vary.

Core Concepts Part 6 Population and Movement Test B

Key Terms 1. death rate 2. infant mortality rate 3. population distribution 4. immigrant 5. living conditions 6. Involuntary 7. sprawl

Key Ideas 8. A 9. D 10. B 11. A

Critical Thinking 12. When the population grows, people use up resources to survive. They cut down forests to get firewood or to open up land for farming. Too much deforestation can lead to the spread of desert-like conditions, which makes it even harder to grow food. Pollution affects the water supply, which can lead to disease and starvation. 13. The population of a country usually increases when the country's birth rate is higher than its death rate. However, if more people move into the country than move out, the country's population will grow. If the difference between the number of

people moving into the country is much larger than the number of people leaving the country, the population can increase significantly. 14. Answers will vary. Possible answer: People living in the rural area would be faced with a decision about whether to migrate or not. They might decide to stay where they were and become part of the suburban neighborhood. On the other hand, those people might feel that they were being pushed out of their homes and their way of life. So they might choose to migrate to another rural area, where they could keep the same way of life.

Essay 15. Answers will vary.

Core Concepts Part 7 Culture and Geography Test A

Key Terms 1. cultural landscapes 2. social structure 3. extended 4. third language 5. ethics 6. cultural diffusion

Key Ideas 7. B 8. B 9. B 10. D

Critical Thinking 11. No, political boundaries and culture regions do not have to match. Earth has thousands of different cultures and culture regions. Culture regions may also extend beyond political boundaries. Latin America is an example of several countries that share a common culture. 12. A culture changes when its cultural traits change. Cultural traits develop and change in places called cultural hearths. Then, traits from cultural hearths spread to surrounding cultures and regions. In general, for a new cultural trait to be adopted by a culture, it must offer some benefit or improvement over an existing trait. An improvement will become part of the culture. 13. Refrigeration made it possible to keep food fresh and safe longer than it would have been without refrigeration. Refrigeration made it possible to ship food long distances—from farms to cities—without the food spoiling. Refrigeration also make it possible for people to buy food and keep it until they are ready to use it.

Essay 14. Answers will vary.

Core Concepts Part 7 Culture and Geography Test B

Key Terms 1. norm 2. nuclear 3. ancestor 4. Muslims 5. traditional religions 6. cultural diffusion

Key Ideas 7. D 8. D 9. C 10. A

Critical Thinking 11. Many of the people who live in the countries in this area are Arab Muslims. That means they practice the religion of Islam and they share other cultural traits. They speak the Arabic language, eat similar foods, and share other cultural traits. 12. Possible answer: Cultural change takes time because many people do not want to change the cultural traits they live with. When a new trait enters a culture, some people may adopt it. Other people prefer to do what they have always done. 13. The two vehicles are made from different materials. The chariot was powered by donkeys, but the car is powered by a gasoline engine. The car can go farther and faster than the chariot can. However, the two vehicles are similar in a number of ways: they both have wheels, they are both convertibles, and both are designed to carry people.

Essay 14. Answers will vary.

Core Concepts Part 8 Government and Citizenship Test A

Key Terms 1. constitution 2. unlimited 3. unitary system 4. foreign policy 5. treaty 6. civic participation

Key Ideas 7. A 8. B 9. B 10. D

Critical Thinking 11. Both governments were democracies in which citizens held political power. Athens was a direct democracy in which citizens gathered to pass laws and choose leaders. The United States is a representative democracy where citizens elect representatives who pass laws. 12. The highest institution of the legislative branch is Congress, the highest office of the Executive branch is the President, and the highest institution of the judicial branch is the Supreme Court. Congress makes laws, the executive branch enforces laws, and the Supreme Court interprets laws and decides their constitutionality. Congress also raises taxes and represents the interests of the citizens. The executive branch also conducts foreign policy, manages daily affairs, and provides for national defense. The judicial branch also settles disputes in courts of law. 13. The United Nations is the largest international organization working for peace, with nearly every country in the world sending representatives to the UN to engage in diplomacy. The UN also seeks to protect the rights guaranteed in the UN Declaration of Human Rights.

Essay 14. Answers will vary.

Core Concepts Part 8 Government and Citizenship Test B

Key Terms 1. limited 2. tyranny 3. federal system 4. diplomacy 5. Civic life 6. interest group

Key Ideas 7. B 8. B 9. B 10. D

Critical Thinking 11. In principle, both forms of government provide order and basic services for their citizens. Limited governments use laws to restrict the authority of government actions. They protect their citizens, provide for their needs, and often give them a voice in changing government. Unlimited governments have no limits on their actions and often fail to protect the basic rights of their citizens. **12.** Both are units of government that apply to regions. A state is simply a region that shares a common government. A nation-state is independent of other states. **13.** Many international relief organizations, such as the International Red Cross, bring relief to countries and regions suffering from conflict. Countries sign treaties such as the Geneva Convention to try to limit the suffering of soldiers, prisoners, and civilians during wartime. And organizations such as the United Nations try to maintain peace and prevent future conflicts.

Essay **14.** Answers will vary.

Core Concepts Part 9 Tools of History Test A

Key Terms **1.** timeline **2.** prehistory **3.** primary source **4.** secondary **5.** anthropology **6.** archaeology **7.** historical map

Key Ideas **8.** B **9.** A **10.** C **11.** D

Critical Thinking **12.** Artifacts would be unlikely to show bias because they were created by people to help them in their lives, not to describe their lives. **13.** Historians study primary sources to understand events from the point of view of the people who experienced them. **14.** They might not have had writing, so it was important to keep track of a society's events through oral traditions.

Essay **15.** Answers will vary.

Core Concepts Part 9 Tools of History Test B

Key Terms **1.** historian **2.** chronology **3.** secondary source **4.** primary **5.** bias **6.** archaeology **7.** anthropology

Key Ideas **8.** D **9.** B **10.** D **11.** B

Critical Thinking **12.** The person creating the source may not remember exactly what happened even though he or she experienced it. Also, the person creating the source may have opinions about the event that lead him or her to leave out or exaggerate information. **13.** Answers will vary. Possible answer: An artifact might tell a historian how people in the society got food or celebrated. **14.** A historian might learn about significant events in the history of a community, or about what the community values.

Essay **15.** Answers will vary.

Chapter 1 The United States Test A

Key Terms **1.** temperate **2.** export

Key Ideas **3.** C **4.** B **5.** A **6.** A **7.** B **8.** C

Critical Thinking **9.** Answers will vary. Students may cite the Rocky Mountains, which cut through a large number of western states and make the area unsuitable for settlement, and the arid climate conditions present throughout much of the Southwest. **10.** As U.S. settlers moved westward in order to fulfill their Manifest Destiny, they pushed Native Americans off their own lands. **11.** U.S. leaders routinely use diplomacy as a non-violent way to negotiate and discuss economic issues and international conflicts with other nations as part of U.S. foreign policy.

Essay **12.** Answers will vary.

Chapter 1 The United States Test B

Key Terms **1.** metropolitan areas **2.** market economy

Key Ideas **3.** A **4.** B **5.** B **6.** B **7.** D **8.** C

Critical Thinking **9.** Both are major mountain ranges in the continental United States. The Appalachians are located in the East and are lower and more rounded than the tall, rugged western Rocky Mountains. **10.** African Americans were originally brought to North America as enslaved people by European colonists. Over time slavery was outlawed, but African Americans still did not receive full rights under the law. The civil rights movement led to the passage of laws that recognized African Americans as having equal rights. **11.** U.S. citizenship gives additional rights to immigrants, such as the right to vote. Becoming a U.S. citizen may also reflect admiration or appreciation for America and its values.

Essay 12. Answers will vary.

Chapter 2 Canada Test A
Key Terms 1. tundra 2. permafrost 3. New France 4. cultural mosaic

Key Ideas 5. C 6. C 7. B 8. A 9. B

Critical Thinking 10. Most Canadians live in urban areas, as do most Americans. Canadian and American rural areas have lower population densities. Many Canadian cities are also located near rivers and other bodies of water, as are American cities. **11.** As Canada grew larger with westward expansion, Britain gave more and more governmental duties directly to Canadians. Canada kept ties to Britain, but its growing population and economic power gave it greater influence as its own country. By the time of the Great Depression, Canada was independent and had to rebuild its own economy in order to become a world power. **12.** Answers will vary. Possible answer: Even if Canada had a less skilled workforce, the country would still possess a large store of natural resources such as minerals and timber. Canada would likely still have a successful economy, but not one as diverse or wealthy.

Essay 13. Answers will vary.

Chapter 2 Canada Test B
Key Terms 1. mixing zone 2. glaciers 3. dominion 4. constitutional monarchy

Key Ideas 5. C 6. A 7. A 8. A. 9. B

Critical Thinking 10. Canada's cities are located in the country's best climate zones. Also, Canada has an advanced economy and many industries, including manufacturing and service industries, which tend to cluster in urban areas. **11.** The Dominion of Canada did not control its own foreign affairs in the same way that the new Canadian government was able to do after 1931, when Britain made Canada fully independent. However, both governments controlled their domestic affairs and both kept strong ties to Britain. **12.** Canada benefits greatly from international trade. One third of its economic activity is made up by exporting natural resources. Trade also benefits Canada by bringing in valued imports.

Essay 13. Answers will vary.

Chapter 3 Mexico Test A
Key Terms 1. altitude 2. aqueducts 3. Mexican Revolution 4. free market

Key Ideas 5. A 6. B 7. C 8. C 9. C

Critical Thinking 10. Most of Mexico's oil is drilled along the country's Gulf Coast. Oil is important to Mexico because it is one of the world's top oil producers, and oil exports bring in a great deal of money for the nation. **11.** A short-term cause was the rigging of the 1910 presidential election by the former Mexican president. The long-term cause was the poverty of many people in Mexico, who watched a small group of Mexicans grow wealthy, controlling most of the land, while the majority worked for little pay, had few rights, and struggled to make ends meet. **12.** Many poor and young people in

Mexico cannot find jobs, and they come to the United States to work. They often send money back to Mexico to support their families. Such remittances provide assistance to many poor families in Mexico and are an important part of Mexico's economy.

Essay 13. Answers will vary.

Chapter 3 Mexico Test B

Key Terms 1. irrigate 2. conquistador 3. Institutional Revolutionary Party 4. remittances

Key Ideas 5. D 6. A 7. B 8. D 9. C

Critical Thinking 10. Baja California is separated from the rest of Mexico by the Gulf of California. Baja California has less fertile land and fewer landform types than the rest of Mexico and is much more narrow. Like northern Mexico, Baja California is very dry. 11. These areas are rich in minerals. Mexico produces more silver than any other country in the world and has large reserves of copper and iron. These resources can be used in Mexican manufacturing or exported to other nations. 12. For the first time since 1929, the Institutional Revolutionary Party lost a presidential election, to a candidate from the National Action Party. Recent victories by PAN candidates suggest that reforms have made Mexico's elections more fair.

Essay 13. Answers will vary.

Chapter 4 Caribbean and Central America Test A

Key Terms 1. Tourism 2. deforestation 3. Maya 4. Santeria 5. ecotourism

Key Ideas 6. B 7. D 8. C 9. B 10. C

Critical Thinking 11. The encomienda was a legal system under which Spanish officials could tax Native Americans or force them to work. In return, the Spanish were to teach the Native Americans Christianity. 12. Widespread poverty in the region causes people to migrate to North America or Europe. 13. Traditional tourism, such as large luxury resorts, uses large amounts of resources while ecotourism seeks to minimize environmental impact.

Essay 14. Answers will vary.

Chapter 4 Caribbean and Central America Test B

Key Terms 1. biodiversity 2. encomienda 3. dictatorship 4. micro-credit 5. Carnival

Key Ideas 6. D 7. B 8. D 9. B 10. A

Critical Thinking 11. Answers will vary. Possible answer: Some people might think the economic benefits are important. Other people might think the presence of many tourists makes life difficult for local people because it increases population density and can lead to water shortages. 12. Some people might have appreciated the economic benefit and other people might have wanted to be independent of foreign influence. 13. Immigrants send money to support their families. Cultural diffusion occurs when people bring their cultural traits, such as food, music, and beliefs, with them.

Essay 14. Answers will vary.

Chapter 5 Caribbean and South America Test A

Key Terms 1. cordilleras 2. *caudillos* 3. austerity measures 4. subsidence 5. insurgents 6. nationalized

Key Ideas 7. C .8. A 9. A 10. D

Critical Thinking 11. Possible answers: European colonists built settlements, established plantations, and dug mines. **12.** Landforms divide the region's population unevenly. The Andes, which are mountainous, have smaller populations made up mostly of mestizos and Native Americans. The Pampas, which have many cities, have larger populations whose residents are mostly of Spanish and Italian descent. **13.** Because of oil, Venezuela has the strongest economy in the region. Profits from oil fund social programs and allow Venezuela to buy a lot of military equipment from Russia. However, Venezuela's economy is dependent on oil exports.

Essay 14. Answers will vary.

Chapter 5 Caribbean and South America Test B

Key Terms 1. ecosystem **2.** terraced farming **3.** El Dorado **4.** paramilitaries **5.** representative democracy **6.** Latin America

Key Ideas 7. B **8.** B **9.** B **10.** C

Critical Thinking 11. There is a variety of climates as a result of the different altitudes of the mountains, and different crops grow well in different climates. For example, bananas and sugar cane can be grown at lower levels and barley, wheat, and potatoes can be grown at higher levels. **12.** Possible answer: Some of the wealthy people with ties to Spain were probably happy with their privileged positions in Caribbean South America and wanted stability maintained by colonial rule. **13.** Answers will vary. Possible answer: Guyana may profit from offshore oil. It will probably be able to export more and bring in more income, thus raising people's standard of living.

Essay 14. Answers will vary.

Chapter 6 The Andes and the Pampas Test A

Key Terms 1. subducted **2.** El Niño **3.** immunity **4.** oligarchy **5.** diversified economy

Key Ideas 6. B **7.** A **8.** C **9.** B **10.** C

Critical Thinking 11. Answers will vary. Possible answer: Buenos Aires has a population of more than 12 million people. It is larger and more densely populated than any other city in the region. Most of the region is not densely populated. **12.** Both countries became industrialized after independence. They also elected leaders who promised to redistribute land to the people. Both countries also experienced revolutions during which their leaders were overthrown by the military. **13.** European influence is one of the key elements that makes the region culturally diverse. There are many mixed race people in countries such as Chile. The dominant language in the region, Spanish, also comes from Europe. However, Native American influence is also strong, and combines with European influence to form a diverse culture.

Essay 14. Answers will vary.

Chapter 6 The Andes and the Pampas Test B

Key Terms 1. vertical climate zones **2.** Altiplano **3.** Mestizos **4.** mercantilism **5.** Bolivia

Key Ideas 6. D **7.** C **8.** B **9.** A **10.** D

Critical Thinking 11. The two largest groups of people in the Andes and the Pampas are indigenous people and mestizos. **12.** Early civilizations were well-organized and sophisticated because they built villages and cities and they organized trade routes. The Incas were especially sophisticated because they expanded their civilization into an empire. **13.** Answers will vary. Possible answer: The system of mercantilism was unfair to people living in the South American colonies. It took their natural resources from them and then forced them to buy goods made from those resources, whether they wanted the goods or not.

Essay **14.** Answers will vary.

Chapter 7 Brazil Test A

Key Terms **1.** Amazon Basin **2.** favelas **3.** export **4.** abolitionists **5.** Ethanol **6.** market economy

Key Ideas **7.** C **8.** B **9.** D **10.** C **11.** C

Critical Thinking **12.** A tropical climate with direct sun, plenty of rain, and humidity supports Brazil's huge rain forest. **13.** During the sugar boom, sugar exports made sugar cane planters wealthy and they controlled the government. Eventually, coffee became an important export, and coffee planters challenged the sugar planters for control. Coffee planters wanted a republic and, along with abolitionists, they formed a new government. **14.** A benefit to cutting down trees is that it clears land for farms and ranching. Since products such as soybeans, meat, and wood are in great demand around the world, cutting down trees allows Brazil to provide these goods. However, there are several drawbacks to destruction of the rain forest. It is a unique place in the world, and its trees absorb carbon dioxide and produce oxygen needed to breathe. Also, the rain forest provides many natural medicines.

Essay **15.** Answers will vary.

Chapter 7 Brazil Test B

Key Terms **1.** savanna **2.** canopy **3.** coup **4.** urban planning **5.** boom | bust **6.** social services

Key Ideas **7.** D **8.** D **9.** B **10.** A **11.** A

Critical Thinking **12.** It is hot and it does not experience great changes in seasons. **13.** Brazil's economy would be strong during a boom period, but when demand and prices for the main export fell, the economy would go into a decline. The boom and bust cycle led Getúlio Vargas to encourage manufacturing, so that Brazil would not be dependent on foreign goods. **14.** Brazil is using ethanol as an alternative fuel for cars. Also, it is starting to do some urban planning to address some of the problems of urban growth. Urban planning has allowed Brazil to create a "green city" that is less harmful to the environment than other cities.

Essay **15.** Answers will vary.

Chapter 8 Ancient and Medieval Europe Test A

Key Terms **1.** direct democracy **2.** patricians **3.** *Pax Romana* **4.** lords | vassals **5.** Crusades

Key Ideas **6.** B **7.** A **8.** C **9.** D

Critical Thinking **10.** The ancient Greeks mainly settled in the valleys with fertile soil near the coast. These settlements were often isolated from each other by mountains or bodies of water, so each settlement became an independent town or city. This isolation eventually lead to the formation of city-states. **11.** Charlemagne changed Europe by uniting much of it under his rule, converting many of the people he conquered to Catholicism, reestablishing the rule of law, and promoting education reform with his school at his palace. **12.** Italian cities served as hubs for goods coming into Europe. Ships from Constantinople and other cities in the Middle East arrived loaded with gold, silks, spices, and other products. Traders loaded these goods onto other ships to send them to other cities in Europe.

Essay 13. Answers will vary.

Chapter 8 Ancient and Medieval Europe Test B

Key Terms 1. city-states 2. philosophy 3. representative 4. Schism 5. economic

Key Ideas 6. C 7. D 8. B 9. B

Critical Thinking 10. In A.D. 312, Roman emperor Constantine I became a Christian. That event—Constantine becoming a Christian—greatly sped up the spread of Christianity in much of Europe. 11. The Christian church sent people across Europe to spread Christianity and gain new members. Gradually, most non-Christians in Europe converted to the Christian religion. As a result, the Christian Church and its teachings were at the center of medieval life all across Europe. 12. The Black Death quickly spread throughout Europe. People from all levels of society died—about 25 million Europeans, by the time the plague ended. Europe faced a labor shortage and a shortage of people with important knowledge and skills. The plague sped up the movement of peasants from manors to the cities. In the cities, those who survived were becoming the new middle class.

Essay 13. Answers will vary.

Chapter 9 Europe in Modern Times Test A

Key Terms 1. perspective 2. northwest passage 3. child labor 4. Treaty of Versailles 5. multinational corporations

Key Ideas 6. A 7. C 8. C 9. A

Critical Thinking 10. Renaissance thinkers questioned religious beliefs and

ancient ideas. They used reason and logic to observe and understand the world around them. Enlightenment philosophers used ideas from the Scientific Revolution, especially observation and logic, to study human nature. They wanted to change society and government. 11. Fast, new machines in factories began to do much of the work once done by people in their homes. Trade increased greatly because workers in factories produced far more goods than individual workers ever had. Industrialized nations needed new places to sell these products. Many of these new markets were in European colonies in the Americas and Asia. 12. Adolf Hitler, like many other Germans, believed that Germany had been treated unfairly after the World War I. After Hitler took control of the government, Germany's economy improved. As a result, many Germans accepted Nazi rule.

Essay 13. Answers will vary.

Chapter 9 Europe in Modern Times Test B

Key Terms 1. movable type 2. triangular trade 3. logic and/or reason 4. fascism 5. democracy

Key Ideas 6. D 7. B 8. D 9. D

Critical Thinking 10. The Columbian Exchange was the exchange of plants, animals, foods, diseases, and ideas between the Eastern and Western hemispheres. European ships carried plants, animals, and diseases to the Americas. The explorers brought food plants, animals, and ideas to Europe. 11. Antidemocratic leaders were able to take power in the Soviet Union because the promise of economic wealth shared among all workers under communism was a very appealing promise. In Italy, nationalist pride led to fascism. In the 1920s, fascist

Benito Mussolini took power in Italy because he promised to build a strong Italian empire. **12.** The Cold War divided Europe into two parts. One was Soviet-controlled communist Eastern Europe. The other was democratic Western Europe, mostly allied with the United States.

Essay 13. Answers will vary.

Chapter 10 Western Europe Test A
Key Terms 1. taiga **2.** air pollution **3.** pound **4.** European Union (EU) **5.** Iberian Peninsula **6.** diversify

Key Ideas 7. C **8.** D **9.** B **10.** A

Critical Thinking 11. Western Europe's most heavily populated areas are located within 100 miles of the coast because most of the coastal areas are on the North European Plain, where it is easier to build cities. Furthermore, the ocean provides many opportunities for trade. **12.** The warm water from the Atlantic Ocean warms the air, which brings mild temperatures to regions as far north as Scandinavia. **13.** On the one hand, German culture includes some of the world's finest music, art, poetry, films, and literature. Germans have also been leaders in the study of botany, mathematics, and military technology. On the other hand, modern German culture is colored by the Holocaust in World War II and the excessive nationalism of the Nazis.

Essay 14. Answers will vary.

Chapter 10 Western Europe Test B
Key Terms 1. urban areas **2.** Gross domestic product (GDP) **3.** reunification **4.** neutrality **5.** cultural diffusion **6.** deportation

Key Ideas 7. D **8.** B **9.** B **10.** A

Critical Thinking 11. The Arctic climate is cold and relatively dry. The Arctic

tundra is a plant community made up of grasses, mosses, herbs, and low shrubs. The Mediterranean climate has mild, wet winters and warm, dry summers. Mediterranean vegetation is a mix of small trees, woodlands, shrubs, and grasses. **12.** During World War II, Nazis wanted to eliminate any groups that did not meet their idea of what German was. Modern Germany teaches tolerance because of its history and its diverse population. Even so, conflict still happens. Some Germans resent immigrants, especially Turks, because they think that immigrants are changing German culture or are taking jobs from Germans. German leaders, recognizing their past, continue to encourage tolerance and open-mindedness. **13.** Answers will vary. Possible answers: Some of the growth in Southern Europe happened because countries such as Spain replaced dictatorships with more democratic forms of government. Entrepreneurs started businesses, large and small companies began to grow and add employees, and privatization of state-owned businesses lowered prices and made the businesses more competitive. Economic growth was also boosted by modernization. At the same time, many of these countries have been moving from making traditional goods, such as textiles, footwear, and porcelain, to developing a service sector that includes telecommunications, financial services, health care, and tourism.

Essay 14. Answers will vary.

Chapter 11 Eastern Europe Test A
Key Terms 1. ice age **2.** capital **3.** secede

Key Ideas 4. B **5.** C **6.** C **7.** D **8.** B

Critical Thinking 9. Religion was restricted under Soviet rule, but after the

breakup of the Soviet Union, religious life has become more active in Eastern Europe. Now, people have more opportunities to start and join religious organizations. With the fall of the Soviet Union, countries in this region have the chance to return to old traditions. 10. The Northern European Plain has a shorter growing season than areas farther south. Large farms are not as common in the southern part of this region. Also, there are more people available to work the land. Many crops such as citrus fruits, olives, and grapes grow well in the warm climate. 11. Most Eastern European countries want to join the European Union because EU membership has economic benefits for its members. Member nations gain access to new trading partners and expanded markets. They also gain more sources for raw materials. Both advantages are important to struggling economies. **Essay 12.** Answers will vary.

Chapter 11 Eastern Europe Test B
Key Terms 1. emigrate **2.** acid rain **3.** cuisine
Key Ideas 4. B **5.** C **6.** B **7.** A **8.** C
Critical Thinking 9. In Eastern Europe, the location of factories depends on the location of natural resources. Because oil and gas are in very short supply, many countries import the oil and gas they need for their industries. As a result, countries like Ukraine, Moldova, and Belarus have become dependent on Russia for their oil and gas imports. **10.** Poland and the Baltic nations of Lithuania, Estonia, and Latvia have been economically successful because they have moved to market economies, created democratic governments, and become members of the European Union. **11.** Violent ethnic conflicts broke out in the Balkan nations after 1991,

sometimes leading to ethnic cleansing. These conflicts disrupted the economies of the countries in this region. Dangerous, unstable conditions made trade difficult. In addition, many people were forced from their homes and had to start new lives in different countries.
Essay 12. Answers will vary.

Chapter 12 Russia Test A
Key Terms 1. Kamchatka Peninsula **2.** steppes **3.** Bolsheviks **4.** KGB **5.** superpower
Key Ideas 6. C **7.** D **8.** C **9.** C
Critical Thinking 10. Russia's most densely populated areas are the regions that have a continental climate, both warm summer and cool summer. The combination of good climate and agriculture in this region has led to the growth of many of Russia's major cities. On the other hand, much of eastern Russia—Siberia—has a subarctic climate. This climate, which has long, very cold winters and short summers, does not support agriculture. As a result, population is sparse in Siberia. **11.** To prevent civil war during World War I, when many peasants were drafted into the army, and created unrest in Russia, the Duma forced Tsar Nicholas II to give up his throne. The Duma formed a temporary government in 1917, and in the fall of that year, Vladimir Lenin and his Bolsheviks took power. This takeover is known as the October Revolution. Lenin and the Bolsheviks promised that his system—communism—would relieve poverty and provide all the goods and services that society needed for everyone to share. **12.** Under communism, the Communist Party makes all the political decisions. The government owns most property and makes most economic decisions. The political leadership requires

Answer Key

party obedience and values party discipline. They also want economic security. Under democratic capitalism, the people and their elected officials make the political decisions. In the market, private producers and consumers make most economic decisions. The political leadership values freedom and prosperity.

Essay 13. Answers will vary.

Chapter 12 Russia Test B

Key Terms 1. Siberia **2.** tsar **3.** soviets **4.** collectivization **5.** censor

Key Ideas 6. C **7.** B **8.** A **9.** D

Critical Thinking 10. Russia's resources include timber, fishing, hydroelectric power, oil and gas, metal ores and minerals. One challenge to the development of all these resources is the great distances separating the resources and markets where they are sold. A second challenge to Russia's resource development is the harsh Siberian climate in which many of these resources are found. **11.** Where some of her predecessors had sought to westernize Russia, Catherine promoted Russian culture. She transformed St. Petersburg into a Russian cultural center. Catherine also expanded Russia by adding some 200,000 square miles to Russian territory, including much of Ukraine and parts of Poland. **12.** Vladimir Putin's economic reforms reduced poverty and led to the emergence of a new middle class, which generally consists of professionals who work in fields related to the global economy. Putin also dramatically expanded Russia's energy industry, exploiting the nation's massive natural resources. As a result, Russia has become a world leader in the production of oil and gas.

Essay 13. Answers will vary.

Practice Test Western Hemisphere
Multiple Choice 1. C **2.** D **3.** C **4.** D **5.**
A **6.** C **7.** B **8.** A **9.** D **10.** B **11.** D **12.**
C **13.** D **14.** B **15.** B **16.** B **17.** B **18.**
B **19.** A **20.** C **21.** A **22.** C **23.** D **24.**
C **25.** B **26.** C **27.** D **28.** A **29.** C **30.**
C **31.** B **32.** C **33.** A **34.** B **35.** A **36.**
C **37.** D **38.** A **39.** B **40.** D **41.** A **42.**
B **43.** C **44.** B **45.** D **46.** A **47.** A **48.**
B **49.** C **50.** D **51.** D **52.** B **53.** D **54.**
B **55.** A **56.** D **57.** D **58.** A **59.** A **60.**
A **61.** A **62.** D **63.** B **64.** C **65.** B **66.**
C **67.** B **68.** A **69** C **70.** A **71.** D **72.**
A **73.** C **74.** D **75.** C **76.** A **77.** C **78.** B

Short Answer 79. Fewer Americans work in agriculture and manufacturing, and many more work in service industries. New technologies have changed the ways Americans work and provided jobs in new areas such as medical research, computers, and technology development. **80.** Both federal governments have officials with separate legislative, executive, and judicial powers. Like the United States, Canada has a federal government where the central government oversees a collection of local governments. Unlike the United States, Canada has strong ties to the British government and uses a parliamentary system in which the legislative branch elects the head of the executive branch. **81.** Free market reforms have opened up Mexico's economy and led to greater growth. Mexican workers once worked mainly in agriculture, but now a majority work in service industries and manufacturing. Foreign investment has increased, as have trading ties with the United States. However, many Mexicans remain poor, especially farmers. Oil remains an important resource for Mexico. **82.** These economies were based on the export of just one or two products, and when world prices for these products

fell, it hurt the economy in the new nations of Caribbean South America. **83.** The Portuguese colonists built settlements in Brazil. They also established sugar cane and coffee plantations and dug mines to extract minerals. **84.** In ancient Rome, society was divided into two basic groups, patricians (wealthy aristocrats) and plebeians (everyone else). Society was also divided between men and women. Fathers had complete control over the home and the family. Only men older than 18 whose parents were both Romans could participate in politics and government. Women worked in the home and, for a long time, had almost no rights. Roman society was further divided between free people and slaves. Slaves were an important part of the Roman economy and everyday life. Slaves could sometimes buy their freedom, and freed slaves could sometimes become Roman citizens. **85.** Answers will vary. Possible answers: One Enlightenment idea that influenced American government was that individuals are born with certain rights, such as life, liberty, and property. Another idea was that the powers of government belong to the people. The people must consent, or give their permission, to be governed. **86.** Larger countries, such as Germany and France, may believe that they have more influence on the policies and laws adopted by the EU. On the other hand, smaller countries may benefit from some of the EU's economic and trade policies. They may want different terms in EU trade agreements than larger countries want. **87.** In Eastern Europe, the location of factories depends on the location of natural resources. Because oil and gas are in very short supply, many countries import the oil and gas they need for their industries. As a result, countries such as Ukraine, Moldova, and Belarus have become dependent on Russia for their oil and gas imports. **88.** Some of Russia's challenges include improving the standards of living of Russian citizens. Alcoholism remains a major problem, and the rates of tuberculosis and HIV/AIDS are very high. All of these problems are indications of the impact of the social and economic upheavals of the 1990s, and they remain problems to be solved.

Essay 89. Maritime climates are found only along coastal areas, next to oceans or seas. As a result, they are moist year-round. Because water warms and cools more slowly than the nearby land, winds that blow from the water onto the shore cool the land a little in summer and warm the land a little in winter. This effect makes the maritime climate milder than climates further inland at the same latitude. Also, wind plays a part in creating the Gulf Stream and the North Atlantic Current, which bring a mild maritime climate to parts of Western Europe that would otherwise have a colder and harsher climate. **90.** Within any society, the family is the most basic unit. Parents and other adults teach children the culture—all the cultural traits—of the society. As long as parents and other adults pass on the cultural traits of the society without any changes, their culture is preserved. As long as people in the society see no benefit in changing cultural traits, families pass on the next generation the cultural traits they have learned, and the culture is preserved. Today, however, people may learn new cultural traits from the mass media, the Internet, by traveling, from immigrants moving to their society, or by migrating themselves to a new homeland. If one individual, or a few individuals, see a new or different cultural trait as an improvement to they way they do things now, they may change. If the change is accepted by more people, the society may change. **91.** Answer will vary. Students should be able to give a general description of the location of their hometown, relative to other major cities or features such as oceans, mountains, and rivers. For the theme of place, students can identify key features of the local population, climate, and industry or agriculture. For the theme of region, students should be able to place their hometown in national region such as the South, Mountain West, Midwest, or Northeast, or at least within a larger area such as the western hemisphere or North America. For movement, students should name any major roads carrying people through their community, list any key exports or imports, and note movements of people such as tourists or immigrants who helped build a community. For human-environment interaction, students have a wide range of possible examples. They might consider how the weather or nearby geographical features such mountains or the ocean affect the lifestyles of people in their hometown. They could give examples of how their community affects the local environment in positive or negative ways. For the conclusion, students should focus on the fact that using all five themes provides a more thorough and complete description of their community than would be possible if any single theme were left out. **92.** Answers will vary. Possible answer: No, because the government in a mixed economy can provide some support: providing jobs, influencing growth, and protecting consumers, for example. Most countries have mixed economies because a pure market economy would not serve all its people best.